God, What's Taking So Long?

E R I K   J A S O N   L A W S O N

God, What's Taking So Long?
ISBN: 978-0-9842534-8-7
Copyright © 2012 by Erik Lawson Ministries

Published by Word and Spirit Publishing
P.O. Box 701403
Tulsa, Oklahoma 74170
wordandspiritpublishing.com

TABLE OF CONTENTS

PART ONE

My soul is in anguish.

How long, O LORD, how long?

—Psalm 6:3 *NIV*

When we pray, sometimes God answers our prayers right away. Yet, at other times, He seems to respond slowly—if He even answers us at all. Why is that?

INTRODUCTION

"God, What's Taking So Long?"

Have you ever asked the question, "God, what's taking so long?"

When you pray, does it sometimes feel like God is using the Pony Express to answer your prayers—even when you've requested FedEx because the answer "absolutely, positively has to be there overnight"?

If so, you are not alone.

Imagine a beautiful flower growing in a garden. This blooming flower represents the answer to one of your prayers.

Maybe you have asked God for your finances to bloom and flourish like this plant. Or maybe you've prayed that any number of important things—your marriage, your kids, your health, your career—would blossom into something beautiful.

God, What's Taking So Long?

SO WHAT'S THE

PROBLEM HERE?

IS THERE

ANYTHING WE CAN

DO TO SPEED UP

THE PROCESS?

But then you go look in your garden, and instead of flourishing beauty, all you see is an ugly mound of dirt.

So what's the problem here? Why does it seem to take so long? Is there anything we can do to speed up the process?

I can tell you that part of the problem is that we live in an instant age—instant messaging, instant cash, instant oatmeal. Someone pointed out to me that now Pop-Tarts have microwave directions—in case your toaster isn't fast enough. Or if you don't have five minutes to mix up that box of mac and cheese, you can now buy instant mac and cheese. Since picking up fast food took too long when you had to get out of your car, they gave us drive-thru windows to speed things up—but if our order takes more than two or three minutes we still get impatient! We like our food processed, but we just don't have time for the process.

Even when we pray, we have been conditioned by our society to expect speed and efficiency—we want to put in our prayer order and get an instant response.

"God bless my finances."
Presto!
"God bless my family."
Presto!

"God bless my health."

Presto!

But that's not how God works. Much of our frustration originates out of a simple misunderstanding about how God operates.

When God created this world, He established the Law of Harvest:

> *While the earth remains,*
> *Seedtime and harvest,*
> *Cold and heat,*
> *Winter and summer,*
> *And day and night*
> *Shall not cease.*
>
> —Genesis 8:22 *NKJV*

The Law of Harvest means that if we want to see a harvest of beauty blooming in our lives, we must plant the seeds into the soil.

There are basically two components of answered prayer.

We are more familiar with the second component, which is the promise of God. If we have a need, God promises to meet that need.

For example, the Bible tells us "God shall supply all your need according to His riches in glory by Christ Jesus"

God, What's Taking So Long?

(Philippians 4:19 *NKJV*). That's the promise of God, and the blooming flower represents that promise.

But the mound of dirt reminds us we can't overlook the first component, which is the Law of Harvest. There is one vital step that must come before we see the promise—we must plant a seed.

Let's say the mound of dirt in the garden represents my finances. What would you think would happen if I just prayed over this dirt, "God, please give me a beautiful flower"?

Would you expect to find a flower there in the next few minutes? Would we see a flower there tomorrow? Next week? Next month?

No.

It won't happen. The Law of Harvest is in effect. Unless somebody plants a seed, there will be no flower.

WE'RE WAITING ON HIM, WHEN THE TRUTH MIGHT BE THAT GOD IS WAITING ON US.

Yet, when we don't see the results we want, we get upset at God. We think that God is taking too long and that we're waiting on Him, when the truth might be that God is waiting on us.

So the first question is not: "Why is it taking so long for my harvest?"

We begin by asking if we have planted the right seeds for our harvest.

CHAPTER ONE

Doing Our Part

Every miracle begins with someone doing his or her part first.

Moses delivered Israel from Egypt, but first Moses had to do what God asked him to do.

Jesus turned water into wine at a wedding, but first the servant had to fill the empty jars with water.

Peter walked on water, but first he had to get out of the boat.

Jesus fed five thousand hungry people, but first the little boy had to give Jesus his lunch.

Miracles occur whenever faith is followed by works. *"But do you want to know, O foolish man, that faith without works is dead? Was not Abraham our father justified by works when he offered Isaac his son on the altar? Do you see that faith was working together with his works, and by works faith was made perfect?"* (James 2:20-22 *NKJV*).

Work follows faith. In the case of Abraham, his work was to obey God by surrendering his son at the altar.

If you're praying for a job, your work may be to pick up a job application, fill it out and turn it in.

If you're single and praying for a spouse, your work may be exercising and getting fit to attract the person of your dreams—or your work may be getting involved in everything you can to meet the other singles at church.

If you're standing in faith for healing, your work might be to start eating right and exercising more.

WE'VE GOT TO MAKE SURE OUR ACTIONS ARE NOT UNDOING OUR FAITH.

We need to do our part—and we've got to make sure our actions are not undoing our faith. I can pray the prayer of faith all day long over my Big Mac, but God isn't going to rebuke the fat grams and the cholesterol just because I prayed!

There are people who are praying in faith for their own safety and protection but by their actions are undoing everything they just prayed for. You can pray, "God protect me while I drive 100 mph in the rain," but let's be realistic—that's not doing your part to cooperate with God.

Years ago I was teaching the teenagers in my youth group about authority and how God places authorities in our life to protect us. One of the examples I used was speed limits—how they were established for our good, and that everyone in the room needed to obey them because lawbreakers were just setting themselves up to get hurt.

One young man turned to his friend after the service and said, "I am not riding with you any more until you stop driving recklessly like Pastor Erik taught us." Two days later the reckless driver asked that same friend to go out with him. Again his friend said, "I am not going driving with you until you obey the Word of God and respect authority." The kid took off without his friend—and a few hours later he lost control of his car while speeding over a hill and died after being ejected from the wreck.

After more than 20 years of ministry and talking with thousands of people, I have observed that one of the most common reasons for delays in answered prayer can be traced to this one issue. We stand on the promises of God, but we ignore the principles of God's Word. The promises of God are His part, but the principles of God are our part—and He'll do His part when we do our part!

"Do not merely listen to the word, and so deceive yourselves. Do what it says.... But the man who looks intently into the perfect law that gives freedom, and continues to do this, not forgetting

AFTER MORE THAN 20 YEARS OF MINISTRY AND TALKING WITH THOUSANDS OF PEOPLE, I HAVE OBSERVED THAT ONE OF THE MOST COMMON REASONS FOR DELAYS IN ANSWERED PRAYER CAN BE TRACED TO ONE ISSUE.

what he has heard, but doing it—he will be blessed in what he does" (James 1:22,25 *NIV*).

God will not overlook His principles to fulfill His promises. An exception might be an act of God's mercy in a crisis situation caused by someone who has spent a long time violating one of God's principles. But this would be an exception and not the norm. Fortunately, if you need mercy, the mercies of the Lord are new every morning (Lamentations 3:22-23).

God asks us to do what we can do, and then He will do what we can't do. *"Do not despise these small beginnings, for the LORD rejoices to see the work begin, to see the plumb line in Zerubbabel's hand"* (Zechariah 4:10 *NLT*).

EACH STEP IS ONE STEP CLOSER TO WHERE WE WANT TO BE AND ONE STEP FURTHER FROM WHERE WE WERE.

The key is to just take one step at a time. Each step is one step closer to where we want to be and one step further from where we were. This is hard for us because we don't want to take one step at a time. We want it the Veruca Salt way—we want it now!

But take a moment to think about how important the process is when you watch an Olympic athlete. You see their success when they stand on the platform and receive their medal—but that isn't when they became a success. It wasn't the event that made them a success. They become a success during the process leading up to the event. The event only reveals the winner; it doesn't make one.

Which of the early morning practices gave that winning Olympian the edge to move up from second to first place?

A split second can separate the first place winner from second place. In one of the winter Olympics downhill ski competitions in the 1970's there was only three-tenths of a second between first and second place! A little bit can make a big difference. The first place winner made over a million dollars in endorsements the following year, while the second place winner made $30,000 as a ski instructor.

In our culture, we are conditioned from birth that to win you have to beat others. To have a winner there must be a loser. If you're not the winner—then you are the loser. But the journey God has set before us isn't the Daytona 500. We're not competing against other people. It is a race against your own potential.

What God Expects

Jesus told a parable about three servants who were each given a sum of money in the local currency, coins called "talents." The master gave the first man five talents, gave the second two talents, and the third one talent.

The first man invested his talents and doubled them. The second man doubled his investment as well. But the third man wanted to protect his capital, so he buried his coin in the ground.

When the master came back some time later, he asked his servants to give account of his money. The first man showed the master he now had ten coins, and the master rewarded him. The second showed the master he now had four coins, and the master rewarded him.

But then the third man returned his original coin, saying, "Lord, I knew you to be a hard man, reaping where you have not sown, and gathering where you have not scattered seed. And I was afraid, and went and hid your talent in the ground. Look, there you have what is yours" (Matthew 25:24-25 *NKJV*).

This servant was afraid because he thought his master would expect something from him that he didn't have the ability to perform. But that's not true at all—God is just looking to see what you do with what He has given you! He'll reward you, not based on what you do in comparison to someone else, but what you do based on what you could have done.

The key is that you get started and begin taking steps today.

There are some things we don't have to wait on God for—things we don't have to pray about. Sometimes God just wants us to get up off our "blessed assurance" and do the things He has already told us to do in His Word.

Doing Our Part

I don't have to pray, "God, should I share my faith?" Jesus already said, "Go." What I do need to pray for is direction on where, with whom, and how to do it.

I don't need to pray, "Should I get involved in a ministry at the church?" I just need to pray about where to get involved.

Some people miss God because they wait too long—when what they really need to do is to start walking. The Bible says, "The steps of a good man are ordered by the Lord" (Psalms 37:23 *NKJV*). God will lead us as we are walking in the direction we sense is right. "We should make our plans, counting on God to direct our steps" (Proverbs 16:9 *LB*).

God not only guides us by steps but also by stops. Paul and his team were headed for Asia and Bithynia when God closed that door, and then He said, "I want you in Greece."

"Now when they had gone through Phrygia and the region of Galatia, they were forbidden by the Holy Spirit to preach the word in Asia. After they had come to Mysia, they tried to go into Bithynia, but the Spirit did not permit them. So passing by Mysia, they came down to Troas. And a vision appeared to Paul in the night. A man of Macedonia stood and pleaded with him, saying, "Come over to Macedonia and help us" (Acts 16:6-9 *NKJV*).

Don't fear missing God's will. If we get off track, Psalm 23 says His staff comforts us. I would rather get out of God's will because I am doing things for God, than miss His will because I am waiting on God. Some churches over-think and over-pray. I ask, "Does it fit the Word? Does it fit our

7

vision? Does it fit our values?" If it does, then let's start taking steps!

Some people wait to start the process until conditions are perfect. But there are no perfect conditions. There is a right time—but don't wait for perfect conditions. The Bible says, "If you wait for perfect conditions, you will never get anything done" (Ecclesiastes 11:4 *NLT*).

Three frogs were sitting on a log. One decided to jump off. How many frogs are left on the log?

Three.

Making the decision to jump isn't the same thing as jumping.

Get started today mapping your route to your dream destinations.

You have a great part to play in your success. Those Christians who think God is going to do everything for them are so heavenly-minded they're no earthly good.

When you look through the Bible you see that we have to do our part before God will do His. James tells us, "Draw near to God and He will draw near to you" (James 4:8). It always starts with us doing our part first. "Give and it shall be given unto you" (Luke 6:38). Every miracle in the Bible began with someone doing his or her part.

In other words, we have to do some work to achieve the success God wants us to have. Salvation is a free gift, but success requires work. You can get to Heaven and be a complete failure. The only place success comes before work is the dictionary.

So why don't more people do the work they need to do to reach their God-given success potential?

Getting to Work

Some people resist work because they think it isn't spiritual. But nothing is more spiritual than doing God's Word. Everything we need for success in any area of life is found in God's Word.

"This Book of the Law shall not depart from your mouth, but you shall meditate in it day and night, that you may observe to do according to all that is written in it. For then you will make your way prosperous, and then you will have good success" (Joshua 1:8 *NKJV*).

A Sunday school teacher was discussing the Ten Commandments with her class of five- and six-year-olds. After explaining the commandment to "honor your father and mother," she asked, "Is there any commandment that teaches us how to treat our brothers and sisters?" Without missing a beat one little boy answered, "Thou shall not kill."

"SUCCESS IS A LITTLE LIKE WRESTLING A GORILLA: YOU DON'T QUIT WHEN YOU'RE TIRED, YOU QUIT WHEN THE GORILLA IS TIRED."

—UNKNOWN

God, What's Taking So Long?

When we do God's Word and what He tells us, that is spiritual. There is more in the Bible to gaining success than just praying for it. There are principles to follow. You can pray for money, but it helps to get a job. "He that doesn't work doesn't eat" (2 Thessalonians 3:10). You can pray to get a wife, but it helps to go where the ladies are. "He that finds a wife finds a good thing" (Proverbs 18:22).

Some people resist work because it's hard. But Jesus never promised being a disciple would be easy—and the Word of God says He will never leave us or forsake us (Hebrews 13:5). A wise man once said, "Success is a little like wrestling a gorilla: you don't quit when you're tired, you quit when the gorilla is tired."

Don't expect success if you're not willing to work for it.

How long will you slumber, O sluggard?
When will you rise from your sleep?
A little sleep, a little slumber,
A little folding of the hands to sleep,

So shall your poverty come on you like a prowler,
And your need like an armed man.

—Proverbs 6:9-11 *NKJV*

THE WAY TO GET TO THE TOP IS TO GET OFF YOUR BOTTOM.

Or as I like to paraphrase that verse: "The way to get to the top is to get off your bottom."

10

Doing Our Part

God promised the children of Israel a land flowing with "milk and honey." But they were shocked when they got there and found the land filled with giants.

But think about that for a moment—if it is good land, wouldn't you expect somebody to already be there? And if it is really good land, wouldn't you expect giants to be living there? But if there is no work involved and no need for battle, then you might wonder why the enemy isn't fighting you for it. As a pastor, I'm not concerned at all by the battles I face—that just tells me Hell fears the church I serve. I get concerned when we're not experiencing battles.

Think about the words "milk and honey." There are no rivers flowing with milk. Where would they get milk? From cattle or goats. You have to get up early and milk them. That is work. God said He was going to bless it, but there is work involved. The word "honey" isn't a reference to honey from a bee but rather jam from figs or dates. To make jam you have to grow fruit, pick it and process it. That takes work. God wants to give us overflowing success—milk and honey—in our families, our finances and our fields, but we will have to work at it.

Parenting takes work. Two brothers were walking home from Sunday school where they had heard some strong preaching on the devil. The younger brother said to the older, "What do you think about all that Satan stuff?" The other boy replied, "Well, you know how Santa Claus turned out. It's probably just Dad."

God, What's Taking So Long?

Marriage takes work. A man found a magic lamp, rubbed it and out popped a genie, who offered to fulfill one wish.

The man said, "I've always wanted to go to Hawaii, but I am afraid to fly and I am afraid of boats. Build me a bridge from California to Hawaii so that I can drive."

The genie replied, "Oh, that's way too much work. Think of a different wish."

"Okay," the man said, "Help me understand women."

The genie paused for a moment.

"You want two lanes or four lanes on that bridge?"

If the grass is greener on the other side of the fence it is only because the neighbors watered their grass. Quit envying the neighbors' lawn and turn on the faucet to water your own.

Remember, God won't do for us what we should do for ourselves. And God won't do for us *before* we do what we should do for ourselves.

Discussion Questions

1. Every miracle begins with someone doing his or her part. When it comes to miracles, what is the relationship between faith and works?

2. The most common reason why our prayers are delayed can be traced to one single issue. What is the relationship between God's principles and God's promises?

3. There are some things we don't have to pray about. Identify several activities we don't need to pray about doing.

4. Sometimes God guides us by steps and sometimes by stops. Can you think of a time or two when God directed you by steps or stops?

CHAPTER TWO

Working with God

There are three kinds of people when it comes to prayer.

First, there are those who pray the promises but don't obey the principles. These are the people who pray about losing weight but never take the stairs.

Second, there are those who obey the principles but don't pray for the promises. This is why good things happen to bad people—they are careful when they climb on ladders because they know that gravity works for sinners as well as saints.

And third, there are those who pray and obey. They know they need God to do His part and they do their part. *"Unless the Lord builds the house, they labor in vain who build it; unless the Lord guards the city, the watchman stays awake in vain"* (Psalm 127:1 *NKJV*).

Notice that if God is not part of the process, our effort is in vain. But you should also notice that there is labor involved. The difference is mostly about our perspective on what we're doing—rather than doing something for God, we are doing something with God. So when we pray, instead of asking God what is taking so long, we should be asking, "God is there a principle in Your Word I am not yet doing?"

Let me show you two quick examples to help you understand how this works in everyday life.

Example #1: Direction

In the first chapter we saw that God leads us in steps. "The steps of a good man are ordered by the Lord," the Bible says, and "He delights in his way" (Psalm 37:23 *NKJV*). Notice that it's not the "leaps" of the righteous that are ordered by God, but his "steps."

Psalm 119:105 says, "Your word is a lamp to my feet and a light to my path." In ancient Israel, people would carry oil lamps or torches at night that would light their steps in the dark. They could only see one or two steps in front of them, but when they would take that step, the next one would be revealed.

In the Old Testament, God spoke to Samuel the prophet and told him to go to Jesse's house in Bethlehem, where he would find and anoint the next king of Israel.

Now the LORD said to Samuel, "How long will you mourn for Saul, seeing I have rejected him from reigning over Israel? Fill your horn with oil, and go; I am sending you to Jesse the Bethlehemite. For I have provided Myself a king among his sons."

And Samuel said, "How can I go? If Saul hears it, he will kill me."

But the LORD said, "Take a heifer with you, and say, 'I have come to sacrifice to the LORD.' Then invite Jesse to the sacrifice, and I will show you what you shall do; you shall anoint for Me the one I name to you" (1 Samuel 16:1-3 *NKJV*).

Notice that God didn't give Samuel all the steps he needed to take. He just gave him enough to get him in the right place for the next step. "You do this," God said, "and then I will show you what to do next." But if Samuel hadn't done what God had shown him, he would have never known what to do next.

IS THERE SOMETHING YOU KNOW THAT GOD TOLD YOU TO DO, BUT YOU HAVEN'T DONE IT YET?

So, if you have been praying for direction in business or marriage and you feel you haven't received God's answer, ask yourself if there is something you know that God told you to do, but you haven't done it yet.

Maybe you have been praying for your marriage and felt you were supposed to join the church marriage group. Have you done it? Maybe you are struggling in your finances, and felt you were supposed to develop a budget. Have you done it?

When I felt it was the right time to start Element Church, God didn't give me all the steps I was supposed to take. I knew I was supposed to move from Tulsa to St. Louis. But I didn't know where to start. And I didn't know where we would get people or money or a building. All I knew was that I was supposed to move to St. Louis. So what would have happened if I had waited until I knew the entire plan for Element Church? I would still be in Tulsa praying. I just had to obey!

Look at what happened when Samuel obeyed God and arrived at Bethlehem.

So it was, when they came, that he looked at Eliab and said, "Surely the LORD's anointed is before Him!"

But the LORD said to Samuel, "Do not look at his appearance or at his physical stature, because I have refused him...

So Jesse called Abinadab, and made him pass before Samuel...Thus Jesse made seven of his sons pass before Samuel. And Samuel said to Jesse, "The LORD has not chosen these" (1 Samuel 16:6-10 *NKJV*).

Notice that when the first son passed by and he wasn't the right one, Samuel didn't stop and say, "Now God, I thought you told me you would show me. What's the deal?" Instead he kept looking. He looked at another son and then the next. He saw seven of Jesse's sons and none of them was the right one. We miss God's will when we stop too soon.

Working with God

And Samuel said to Jesse, "Are all the young men here?" Then he said, "There remains yet the youngest, and there he is, keeping the sheep."

And Samuel said to Jesse, "Send and bring him. For we will not sit down till he comes here." So he sent and brought him in. Now he was ruddy, with bright eyes, and good-looking. And the Lord said, "Arise, anoint him; for this is the one!" (1 Samuel 16:11-12 *NKJV*).

Often God will show you the right thing to do by closing the door on the wrong thing.

After I moved to St. Louis, I knew I wanted Element Church to be in the O'Fallon/Wentzville area. So then I did what we all do when starting a church—I looked into renting a school for the Sunday services. But all the doors kept closing to me. When it appeared that none of the schools were available, I got frustrated and said, "God, I thought You wanted me here to start Your church, but nothing seems to be opening up."

Then my wife said, "What about the YMCA in Chesterfield?"

So I drove over to look and it was exactly what we needed! It was a great place and the price was cheaper than a school.

So if you're trying to move forward and all the doors keep closing, just keep doing what you

TOO OFTEN WE DON'T SEE THE PROMISE BECAUSE WE'VE QUIT TOO SOON.

know to do. Too often we don't see the promise because we've quit too soon.

Example #2: Singleness

When I was single I stood on the promises of God. I had two favorite scriptures:

> *"He who finds a wife finds what is good and receives favor from the LORD."*
>
> —Proverbs 18:22 *NIV*

> *"Now to him who is able to do immeasurably more than all we ask or imagine, according to his power that is at work within us..."*
>
> —Ephesians 3:20 *NIV*

I was praying one day and God said, "Erik, let's talk about those verses you're standing on. What does your first verse say?"

"He who finds..."

God stopped me right there. "How do you find something? You look for it! How can I help you find a wife when you are doing nothing to look?"

I had to admit that I wasn't looking very hard. Even if a girl

EVEN IF A GIRL SHOWED UP AT MY FRONT DOOR IN A WEDDING DRESS I'D PROBABLY SLAM THE DOOR.

showed up at my front door in a wedding dress I'd probably slam the door.

Then God said, "You are praying for a wife that is exceedingly abundantly above all you can ask or think, and I am able to do that. But when this girl sees you, will she think you are exceedingly abundantly above all she can ask or think?"

God didn't even wait for my answer.

"Burn that flannel shirt," He said. "Start taking care of yourself. You say you want to manage a marriage, but can you manage yourself? Why should I give you My daughter if you can't take care of her?"

Our first question shouldn't be, "God, what is taking so long?" Instead, we should start by asking, "God is there a principle in Your Word I am not yet doing?"

WE SHOULD START BY ASKING, "GOD IS THERE A PRINCIPLE IN YOUR WORD I AM NOT YET DOING?"

Discussion Questions

1. God doesn't always give us His entire plan at one time—often He just gives us our next step. Is there anything that God is leading you to do that you haven't done yet?

2. Answered prayer is the result of us doing our part and God doing His part—and our part is to "pray and obey." Can you think of any instances when you suspect your prayers were hindered because you prayed but didn't obey, or you obeyed but didn't pray?

3. Can you recall an occasion in your life when God led you by "opening a door"? Have there been occasions when God has directed you by "closing a door" in your life?

4. When the answer to a specific prayer seems to be delayed, it may be helpful to "trouble-shoot" your prayer request by looking at the promises and principles involved. If you are waiting on the answer to a prayer right now, are there any principles involved that you are not yet doing?

CHAPTER THREE

Why We Wait

Why does God make us wait? If He created the whole world in six days, why does it take six months—or six years—to get that answer we have been praying for?

One little boy who always seemed to get into mischief began praying that God would help him become a better boy. After a few days he didn't see any change, so he prayed, "Lord, if You're having a hard time making me a better boy, don't worry about it—I'm having a real good time like I am."

Sometimes *we're* the reason we're waiting for answers to our prayers.

"I'm doing all the principles I know to do," you say, "but I'm still not seeing the promises. What else can I do?"

Maybe you've already done enough.

Let's say I want to grow a flower. I know the Law of Harvest tells me that the first step is to plant seed in the ground and the second step is to wait.

God, What's Taking So Long?

So I plant a seed one morning and then wait overnight.

In the morning I don't see a flower. I get concerned, so I dig up the seed to see if there's a problem. The seed appears to be fine. I put it back in the ground. This time I add a little Miracle-Gro.

Later in the afternoon, I check again and there's still no flower! So I dig up the seed. It still looks good. Now I'm really getting frustrated. I fall to my knees and cry out to the heavens, "Oh God, what is taking so long?"

Sometimes we get impatient when we don't see results overnight. The truth is that God promises us a harvest when we are faithful to plant the seed. But with the process of harvest we also have to wait. Seeds take time to grow.

"We do not want you to become lazy, but to imitate those who through faith and patience inherit what has been promised" (Hebrews 6:12 *NIV*).

There are times we just have to be patient.

WAITING IS ONE OF GOD'S GREATEST TOOLS FOR SPIRITUAL GROWTH.

Sometimes we start by doing the right thing, and then after a while we begin to wonder why we're not seeing an instant change—and so we stop doing the right thing. This kind of inconsistency in obeying the principles is one of the great hindrances to seeing the promises come to pass in our lives.

At other times God makes us wait because of what waiting does inside of us. Waiting is one of God's greatest tools for spiritual growth. It's like going to the spiritual gym.

When you get on the treadmill, you may feel like you are doing a lot but are getting nowhere. But the truth is that something is taking place inside you. Does waiting feel like you're carrying a heavy weight in your life? Think of it as pumping iron for your spiritual development.

There's also another way that spiritual development is like going to the gym. You know how some people sign up for a gym membership, but then rarely use it? They like the idea of getting results, but they're not committed to working out.

When we gave our lives to Christ, we received complimentary spiritual fitness memberships. God wants to transform us into the image of Christ. But too many of us carry the membership card, even though we're not committed to the spiritual development that comes with it. So God says to us, "I know that you might not be consistent at going to the gym for your spiritual fitness development, so I am sending the spiritual gym to you. You can walk the treadmill and lift the weights of waiting in the convenience of your own home."

IF YOU ARE WAITING FOR AN ANSWER TO PRAYER AND YOU FIND YOURSELF LOSING STRENGTH, YOU MIGHT BE WAITING ON THE WRONG THING.

You may not always enjoy the workout at the time, but something is taking place inside you.

Waiting Renews Our Strength

"But those who wait on the Lord shall renew their strength; they shall mount up with wings like eagles, they shall run and not be weary, they shall walk and not faint" (Isaiah 40:31 *NKJV*).

There will be times when you will run out of strength and you will have to take time to renew your energy. You are not the Energizer Bunny. (Once I sat in a church service with the Energizer Preacher—he just kept going and going and going.) But when our strength is faltering, we can renew our strength by waiting on the Lord.

For me sometimes waiting in a line or a reception area feels like it is sucking the strength out of me. But if you are waiting for an answer to prayer and you find yourself losing strength, you might be waiting on the wrong thing.

WAITING ON THE ANSWER AND WAITING ON GOD ARE TWO DIFFERENT THINGS.

If you have the Burger King Bible—the "Have It Your Way" translation—then Isaiah 40:31 reads, "But those who wait on the *ANSWER* shall renew their strength."

But my Bible says, "Those who wait on the *LORD* shall renew their strength."

Why We Wait

Waiting on the answer and waiting on God are two different things. When you pray, you should ask yourself, "Am I waiting on the answer or am I waiting on the Lord?" We need to make our waiting less *goal*-oriented and more *God*-oriented. The difference is our focus—one is about God, the other is about the answer.

So how does waiting on the Lord renew our strength?

Have you ever been waiting on something and it seemed like it was taking forever? You could feel every second tick by. Often doctors' offices feel that way for me. If a doctor ever asks me, "What would you do if you only had one day to live?" I'm going tell him I will spend it sitting in his lobby waiting for my appointment because then it would be the longest day of my life!

However, have you noticed how fast time flies when you are in the presence of someone you love and enjoy being with? Think back to when you were first in love. How fast time went when you were with them! It felt like the hours passed by in minutes.

Why is that?

It's about focus. Of course time moves at the same pace for everyone, but it sure feels different depending upon what you are focused on.

So if we are waiting on an answer from God and time seems to be moving at a snail's pace, let that be an internal indication that our focus is in the wrong place. But when our focus is God—when we are in His presence and enjoying His love—time flies!

Waiting Refines Our Character

"More than that, we rejoice in our sufferings, knowing that suffering produces endurance, and endurance produces character, and character produces hope" (Romans 5:3-4 *ESV*).

GOD WILL TAKE OUR WEAKEST AREAS AND TURN THEM INTO OUR GREATEST STRENGTHS.

Have you seen a child who got everything they wanted and never had to wait or work for anything? How did that kid turn out? A child who never learns to wait lacks something in character.

God will take our weakest areas and turn them into our greatest strengths. He did this in the lives of the great leaders in the Bible—their greatest weaknesses became their greatest strengths.

Abraham is known as the "father of faith." But twice, when he was faced with tight situations, he told his wife to lie and say she was his sister. If you go through Abraham's life, you'll see time after time where he blew it in terms of unbelief. You'll see how once he got impatient and created an Ishmael. Yet, he is best known for his great faith.

Moses was one of only two people in the Bible ever called "meek"—and Jesus was the other. But we see that Moses' biggest problem was anger management. At the beginning of his career he got angry and killed the Egyptian. Near the end he got angry and struck the rock. It was his anger problem that kept Moses out of the Promised Land. Yet, he is best known for his meekness.

John, who wrote the book of John and three letters, is known as the "beloved apostle of love." But before Jesus got ahold of him, John's nickname was "Boanerges," which means, "Son of Thunder." One day when some people didn't want to listen to Jesus, he said, "Lord, why don't we just call down hell-fire on those people!" Yet, he is best known for his love.

Simon was wishy-washy. He was always running around, putting his foot in his mouth. He would impulsively jump out of a boat to walk on water and start to sink. He was quick to say, "Lord, I'll never deny You," and then he did it three times in a row! Yet, he is best known by the name Jesus gave him—"Peter," which means "Rock."

The Christian life can be summed up as character development. We grow in character gradually, not by our own power but through God's grace that works in us while we are waiting.

I remember complaining to God one time that something I was going through wasn't very comfortable. The Holy Spirit spoke to my heart: "I am more concerned with your character

SOMETIMES THE THING WE ARE PRAYING FOR IS BIGGER THAN OUR CHARACTER CAN HANDLE.

than your comfort. Character now might bring greater comfort, but comfort at the expense of character ultimately brings lasting discomfort."

Sometimes the thing we are praying for is bigger than our character can handle. So God first works on our character to handle the responsibility of our answer.

For example, when I was eighteen I thought I was ready to get married. But God had me wait. He had work to do. It turns out that Christy was only thirteen when I was eighteen, which is wrong and illegal (except in certain southern states). But more than that, I thought I was ready for marriage—but God knew better. When I was twenty-four and Christy was nineteen we finally got married, and even then our first year was awful, mostly due to my lack of maturity.

Life's journey is more than a destination. It is about who I have become in the journey, and who I am when I arrive at the end of my life. And that comes down to my character.

ONE MEASUREMENT OF MY CHARACTER IS WHAT WOULD I DO IF I THOUGHT I WOULD NEVER GET CAUGHT.

God is always working on our character. Our reputation is who people say we are, but our character is who we really are when no one is looking. One measurement of my character is what would I do if I thought I would never get caught.

Martin Luther King Jr. put it this way: "Cowardice asks the

question, 'Is this safe?' Consensus asks, 'Is this popular?' Conscience asks, 'Is this right?'"

Usually the right thing isn't the easy thing, but it is still the right thing. There are times it doesn't seem to pay to do the right thing, but we do it because it is right.

A few years ago a girl found a wallet containing $224, and when she returned it, as a reward she received a single lottery ticket. Sometimes doing the right thing doesn't seem to pay, but in the long run it always does. The reward may be immediate, and at other times it may take a while. In this girl's case, the lottery ticket paid out $45,000.

The tests, challenges and struggles we face in life are construction zones where God pulls the jackhammer out and tears up old crusty concrete and pours into our heart new solid foundations. Trials can be difficult but we can trust God to help us in these times. The Bible says we are to count it all joy.

"My brethren, count it all joy when you fall into various trials, knowing that the testing of your faith produces patience. But let patience have its perfect work, that you may be perfect and complete, lacking nothing" (James 1:2-4 *NKJV*).

We're not thanking God for the pain caused by our trials, but we are thanking Him that He has the answer and is helping us get through it.

It is this process that builds character.

No pain, no gain.

God, What's Taking So Long?

It is a long and difficult struggle for a butterfly larva to break free of its cocoon. If you felt sorry for a baby butterfly and tried to help by opening his cocoon for him, you would cause deadly harm. He would emerge weak and unable to open his wings and would soon die or be eaten by a predator.

It is the process of the struggle that gives the butterfly the strength to spread his wings and fly.

Sure, it would feel better in the short term if our lives were free from struggles, but in the end, without our struggles, we would fail to become the strong followers of Christ we need to be.

Discussion Questions

1. What is the difference between waiting on an answer and waiting on God—and why is this distinction important?

2. Sometimes by praying you've already done enough. In what ways can prayer be compared to planting a seed?

3. Inconsistency is one of the great hindrances to answered prayer. Identify one of your specific prayer requests and describe what consistency and inconsistency might look like.

4. We see that the process of waiting on God refined the character of many people in the Bible—and often their greatest weaknesses became their greatest strength. Is there a weakness in your life that you'd like to see become your greatest strength?

CHAPTER FOUR

Profiting from Our Problems

Paul tells us there are two things we can do when we bring our problems to God that will speed up the answers to our prayers: *"Do not be anxious about anything, but in everything, by prayer and **petition,** with **thanksgiving,** present your requests to God"* (Philippians 4:6 *NIV*).

First, we need to bring our requests to God by petition.

Perhaps you've signed a petition or even been involved in collecting the signatures of people who agree on some issue, and then that document is passed along to the appropriate authorities. It's essentially the same when we petition God. We find where the Word of God agrees with our request, and then we bring that before God.

"Now this is the confidence that we have in Him, that if we ask anything according to His will, He hears us. And if we know that He hears us, whatever we ask, we know that we have the petitions that we have asked of Him" (1 John 5:16-17 *NKJV*).

IT IS IMPORTANT THAT WE SPEND TIME READING GOD'S WORD EVERY DAY SO WE CAN KNOW ALL OF HIS PROMISES FOR US.

Our petition to God is based upon His Word—which is His will—and contains the one signature we need—the name of Jesus. When we pray in this way, we are praying God's promises back to Him. That is why it is important that we spend time reading God's Word every day so we can know all of His promises for us.

Second, we need to bring our requests to God with thanksgiving.

No matter how painful the trial or stressful the situation, God says we can bring everything that concerns us to Him—and He will turn it around to our benefit. We can express our gratitude and thanksgiving freely, knowing that when we give a problem to God, He will work it to our good.

According to Harper's Index, the average American is in a bad mood 110 days out of the year. Some are below average, some are above average, but this report suggests that people are generally in a bad mood about 30 percent of the time.

But we can walk in peace and thanksgiving all the time, even in the middle of stressful problems.

"My brethren, count it all joy when you fall into various trials, knowing that the testing of your faith produces patience. But let patience have its perfect work, that you may be perfect and

complete, lacking nothing" (James 1:2-4 *NKJV*).

Peace does not mean problem-free living, because we're always going to have problems. Peace does not mean the absence of conflict, because we will always have conflicts. Peace does not mean everything always goes your way, because it won't. If our peace of mind depends upon circumstances going our way, then we are going to be constantly up and down.

We can pray with thanksgiving because we know that God will work out all things for our good. We don't thank Him for the problem, but we thank Him for the answer—and we thank Him for turning our problems into profit.

THE AVERAGE AMERICAN IS IN A BAD MOOD 110 DAYS OUT OF THE YEAR. GENERALLY PEOPLE ARE IN A BAD MOOD ABOUT 30 PERCENT OF THE TIME.

1. Problems Direct Us

Sometimes we can get off course in our lives and God will use a problem to direct us to take the next step. "When everything is coming your way," Larry the Cable Guy said, "you're in the wrong lane!"

The Bible tells about the time Elijah was in the middle of the desert, waiting for God beside a brook. He was there for quite a while, but God had provided plenty of resources to keep him alive—the brook supplied him with water to drink, and ravens brought him food. Everything was going great until one day the brook dried up.

Have you ever had a brook dry up in your life?

Elijah didn't get mad about it. He didn't say, "God, why is this happening?" He simply sought God for his next step. And God gave it to him.

God may be using the situations in your life to show you your next step. Some people won't move unless they experience a little pain. C.S. Lewis said, "God whispers to us in our pleasure but He shouts to us in our pain."

God quickly gets our attention when problems come upon us.

2. Problems Inspect Us

God also uses problems in our lives to teach us about ourselves. Have you ever learned anything about yourself through a problem? I bet you have. God can use all sorts of situations to reveal our weaknesses or character faults. God may even allow a problem in our lives to show us a blind spot.

A concerned husband went to the family doctor. "I think my wife is losing her hearing," he said. "She never hears me the first time I say something. In fact, I often have to repeat things to her over and over again. It is really getting irritating."

"Well," the doctor replied, "Go home tonight, stand about fifteen feet behind her and say something. If she doesn't reply, move five feet closer and say it again. Keep doing this until she responds, so we can get an idea of the severity of her deafness."

Sure enough, the husband goes home, and he does exactly as instructed. He stands fifteen feet behind his wife, who is standing in the kitchen, chopping some vegetables. He said, "Honey, what's for dinner?"

He gets no response, so he moves about five feet closer and asks again.

"Honey, what's for dinner?" No reaction.

He moves five feet closer and tries again. Still no reaction.

Then he moves up to stand right behind her—about an inch away—and asks again, "Honey, what's for dinner?"

"For the third time," she said, "vegetable stew!"

3. Problems Correct Us

When problems arise, maybe "Why is this happening?" is the wrong question. Instead, you might want to ask, "What do you want to teach me?"

God may want to teach you something about Himself through this problem. Maybe He wants to teach you about His power. Maybe He wants to teach you that you can trust Him to handle any situation.

At times our problems overwhelm us like a dense fog and we see no way out. But we need to see things the way God sees them. Fog can blanket a city for seven blocks and be 100 feet deep, but if all that fog could be gathered and changed into water, it would fill only one glass.

Sometimes when we see our problems for what they really are, we discover they are nothing more than a single glass of H_2O.

4. Problems Protect Us

I read in the paper a few years ago about a man who was running late to catch his plane because he got a flat tire on the way to the airport. At the time he was very upset that he missed his flight, but it turns out he had missed the Value Jet flight that tragically crashed into the Florida Everglades.

GOD IS ALWAYS WORKING ON SOMETHING BIGGER FOR US. OFTEN THE LONGER THE WAIT, THE BIGGER IT IS.

Sometimes what looks like a problem may actually be a blessing in disguise—and protects you from a much bigger problem.

5. Problems Perfect Us

God uses problems to burn off the impurities. *"See, I have refined you, though not as silver; I have tested you in the furnace of affliction"* (Isaiah 48:10 *NIV*).

Profiting from Our Problems

A man asked a silversmith how he knew when the silver was pure. The silversmith said, "When I see my reflection in it." When God can see His reflection in you, He knows He's burned off the impurities.

God is always working on something bigger for us. Often the longer the wait, the bigger it is.

"As you know, we consider blessed those who have persevered. You have heard of Job's perseverance and have seen what the Lord finally brought about. The Lord is full of compassion and mercy" (James 5:11 *NIV*).

There's a great story in the Bible about a woman named Hannah who was praying—and waiting—for children. And to make things more difficult for Hannah, her husband had another wife who was having children regularly.

Mark Twain was once pushed into an argument with a Mormon acquaintance on the issue of having multiple wives. The Mormon demanded that Twain cite any passage of Scripture expressly forbidding polygamy.

"Nothing easier," Twain replied. "No man can serve two masters."

The Bible says that the other wife was not kind to Hannah and constantly provoked her. How would you feel? You're doing everything you can to have children to no avail, all the while your husband's other wife keeps saying, "I got me another baby, Hannah! How about you?"

God, What's Taking So Long?

This happened year after year. Every year Hannah would go to the temple and talk to God about it: "God, I pray that you would give me a child."

And she waited and waited and waited and waited.

Eventually, after many prayers and much waiting, God gave her the answer to her prayers—Hannah gave birth to a boy. We never hear the name of any of the other wife's kids, but we do know the name of Hannah's son. His name was Samuel, and he became a great prophet in Israel, and he got two books of the Bible named after him.

Why did God make Hannah wait? While Hannah was waiting, God was developing her. She was developing patience. She was developing a prayer life and a deep trust in God. In order for Hannah to develop a Samuel, God first had to develop a Hannah. And He did that *during* her time of waiting. He developed her character *through* this time of waiting.

Discussion Questions

1. We know that only good gifts come from God (see James 1:17, Matthew 7:11). So how can we present our prayer requests to God "with thanksgiving," but avoid thanking God for giving us the problem?

2. The Bible promises us peace "that surpasses all understanding" (Philippians 4:7). Is it possible to experience that peace and still have problems in your life? How would that work?

3. Sometimes our problems "inspect us" or "correct us" or "perfect us." Can you think of an instance when God has used a problem in your life to teach you something about yourself or reveal something about Himself?

4. Sometimes our problems "protect us" or "direct us." Can you think of an instance when God has used a problem in your life to uncover or prevent a bigger problem? Has God ever used a problem to get your attention so that He could show you the next step in your life?

CHAPTER FIVE

Opening the Door
to Blessing

Have you ever met someone who prayed and didn't get an answer to that prayer and then got mad at God? Let's bring that question a little closer to home. Have you ever prayed and didn't get an answer to your prayer and you got mad at God?

Here is another question. Does God promise to answer every prayer?

No. He does not.

Did that answer come as a shock to you? God is not obligated to answer any of our prayers. Scripture lays out clear conditions for the prayers that God will answer.

Some people have given up on prayer because they have prayed and it didn't seem to work. But just because it didn't work for someone once doesn't mean it doesn't work for anyone ever!

God, What's Taking So Long?

DOES GOD

PROMISE TO

ANSWER EVERY

PRAYER?

Have you ever been locked out of your home or your car? Did you stop using doors? Did you give up on the whole door thing—are you now a windows-only person? Or did you realize that just because you were locked out once doesn't mean doors don't work—it just means you didn't have the right key!

Several years ago I pulled into our driveway at home and realized I had our spare set of keys—and that I had taken the house key off and hadn't put it back on! So there I was, stuck on the porch, locked out of our house for two hours on a hot, muggy day as I waited for my wife to get home.

When she got home I told her I was locked out.

"Why didn't you use the key?" she asked.

I told her I had taken the key off and hadn't put it back on.

"But I put it back on," she said. "Didn't you look at the keychain?"

I was locked out—yet I had the key the whole time!

There are many people who pray wrong and don't get results. Rather than checking to see if they are using the right key, they're getting mad at God and giving up on prayer because they think it doesn't work.

We Must Be Right with God

Jesus said, *"If you abide in Me, and My words abide in you, you will ask what you desire, and it shall be done for you"* (John 15:7 *NKJV*).

Notice that we must abide in Him to receive answers to our prayers. Obviously this doesn't mean we have to be perfect, or none of us would ever have any of our prayers answered. In fact, many of our prayer needs are the result of our imperfections.

But abiding in Him means that we are doing our best to live for Him.

There are people who don't know Christ, however. They are living their lives apart from God. But then, when they get into a crisis, they begin to pray—and then they get mad when God doesn't answer! Let me ask you a question: Is God obligated to answer the prayer of someone who isn't living for Him?

Let's say there is a runaway teenager who lives under a bridge down the road from me. He is in rebellion against the law and living however he wants.

Then one day I meet him and offer to adopt him and bring him into my family and give him all the rights and privileges of being my child.

But he refuses. "I don't want to live under the rules of your house," he snarls. "I want to be free to be my own person and make my own decisions."

Because I am a generous person, I begin putting out food for him every day. Whenever I see him I reach out to him and continually give him opportunity after opportunity to come live with me.

But he always refuses.

Then one day he gets sick. He knows I can afford the medicine he needs to feel better, so he stops by my house to ask for help.

"I don't want a relationship with you," he growls. "I don't want to live by your rules. I don't even like you. I plan to continue making fun of everything you stand for. But I do want your money to buy medicine to help me get better, so I can go back to living my own life without needing you or thinking about you."

Do I have an obligation to give him anything?

In fact, is it possible that I might be hurting him more by helping him because I am enabling his destructive behavior? Perhaps the best thing for him would be to let him hit rock bottom.

YOU'LL HEAR PEOPLE SAY, "WE'RE ALL CHILDREN OF GOD," BUT THAT'S NOT REALLY TRUE.

Whether or not we've hit rock bottom, God shows us His mercy day after day! We don't deserve it, but He gives us everything good. He's not obligated to do anything for us, but He has adopted us into His family!

Opening the Door to Blessing

You'll hear people say, "We're all children of God," but that's not really true. We are all the creation of God, but not everyone is a child of God. It is only when we accept Christ as our Savior that we are adopted into His family and receive the rights and privileges of being His children.

Some people in the family of God are running away from home and still expect God to answer their prayers. They run away, and then come home to get more stuff, just to run away again. Should God keep giving them the stuff that enables them to run away? If you are a runaway, God doesn't owe you an answer until you return home and then He expects you to stay home! (See Luke 15 for a story about a prodigal son.)

When my uncle was two years old, he walked into the living room wearing nothing but his underwear, as little boys love to do. He had a little potbelly, an outie belly button and a fair complexion. In those days furnaces were big and bulky and got really hot. My uncle was getting too close to the heater so his mother said, "Mark, get away from the furnace or you will burn yourself!" So he took a few steps back from the furnace, put out his belly and then ran right smack into the burning furnace. He doesn't remember what he was thinking at the time, but he burned himself real badly.

Scripture tells us that it is our own poor choices that spoil our lives. *"A man's own folly ruins his life, yet his heart rages against the LORD"* (Proverbs 19:3 *NIV*).

Rather than taking responsibility for our own actions, we often blame God. That would be like my uncle saying, "God, if you really loved me, how could you let me get burned like this?"

But throughout the Bible, God warns us about things—"Don't touch the furnace because it is hot!"—and then we stick out our little bellies and run full steam ahead into the furnace and get burned, and then we get mad at God. Much of the stress in life that we complain to God about can be traced back to our own disobedience.

> DISOBEDIENCE IS ONE OF THE GREAT CAUSES OF STRESS IN OUR LIVES.

Disobedience is one of the great causes of stress in our lives.

The good news is that God does care about us and He is willing to help us out of our mess. Unfortunately, too many people just want God to help them get out of the stress, but don't want to give up what got them in the mess. Their prayer is, "God, I want to keep disobeying You, and I want you to bless my disobedience."

Well, that isn't how it works. God will just sit on the sideline and let you stress out—until you've had enough and you're ready to return to Him.

If we were to live completely within God's boundaries, we would dramatically reduce stress in our lives. When we live outside those boundaries, we create stress for ourselves. When a husband doesn't love his wife, there will be stress in the marriage. When parents go against God's Word in raising their children, there will be stress. When a couple goes against God's Word in managing their finances, there will be financial stress. Disobedience always brings stress.

We Must Pray in the Name of Jesus

Jesus said, *"And whatever you ask in My name, that I will do, that the Father may be glorified in the Son"* (John 14:13 *NKJV*).

What is so special about Jesus' name? For years I had no idea. I'd hear everybody pray and they'd end their prayers, "In Jesus's name, amen." I thought it was a spiritual sign-off, like a trucker on a CB radio—"Ten-four, good buddy!"

When we pray and use the name of Jesus, we are using His line of credit with the Father—and that's good news, because our credit is shot! Whenever we receive an answer to our prayer, it's not because we are worthy—it's because He is worthy! Jesus is our American Express Platinum card. *"Until now,"* Jesus said, *"you have asked nothing in My name. Ask, and you will receive, that your joy may be full"* (John 16:24 *NKJV*).

We Must Pray in Faith

If you are constantly feeling stressed out, you are carrying something that is not yours to carry. God is saying, "Let me carry that for you." Are you carrying something that doesn't belong to you right now? Give it to God in prayer and leave it with Him—and don't take it back.

Prayer reveals what we believe about God. My prayer life—or the lack of it—reveals what I really believe about God. When I go to everyone else about my problem before I go to God, that reveals my lack of faith in God's ability.

Three men were hiking and came to a violent, raging river. They needed to get to the other side but they had no idea how they were going to get across.

So the first guy prayed, "God, give me strength to get across this river," and *poof!* God gave him big arms and big legs and he swam across the river.

The second guy thought he'd try praying, too. He prayed, "God, give me strength and ability to get across the river," and *poof!* God gave him a rowboat and he rowed across the river.

The third guy saw how well this was working. He prayed, "God, give me strength and ability and intelligence to get across the river," and *poof!* God turned him into a woman. She looked at the map, found the bridge, and walked across the river.

There's only one kind of prayer that God answers—the prayer of faith.

When Jesus healed the two blind men He touched their eyes and said, "According to your faith let it be to you" (Matthew 9:29 *NKJV*).

In fact, when we are not in faith, God can't move on our behalf.

When Jesus was in His hometown, the Bible says "because of their unbelief, he couldn't do any mighty miracles among them except to place his hands on a few sick people and heal them. And he was amazed at their unbelief" (Mark 6:5-6 *NLT*).

What is faith?

"I believe that God can do it."

That's fact, not faith.

"I believe God might do it."

That's hope, not faith.

"I believe God will do it."

That's still hope, because it's future tense.

Faith believes that God has done it! Faith believes that when I pray, God answers. And faith believes I have the answer—even though I don't see it right now!

A six-year-old girl had been so naughty all week that her mother decided to punish her by not letting her go to the Sunday School picnic. When the day came, the mother felt she had been too harsh and changed her mind. But when she told the little girl she could go to the picnic after all, the child seemed angry and upset.

"What's the matter?" her mother said, "I thought you'd be happy to go to the picnic."

"It's too late," the little girl said. "I've already prayed for rain."

I think that if God answered some people's prayers they'd have a heart attack. He probably hasn't answered some of their prayers just to keep them alive.

We see so little in our lives because we expect so little. Jesus didn't say, "according to your ability," or "according to your education," or "according to how good a person you are"—He said, "According to your faith let it be to you."

Faith is the number one prerequisite in answered prayer. I meet people all the time who tell me, "I prayed in faith and didn't see an answer, so this prayer of faith must not work." I always remind them that our faith is based on the character of God—not on the results we see. So even if I pray and don't get results, it doesn't change my faith, because my faith is in God.

I have prayed the prayer of faith over sick people and seen them get healed. I prayed the prayer of faith over a man killed in a car accident and saw him come back to life. I prayed the prayer of faith over a little boy who was accidentally shot in the head by a friend with a .22 and he lived, even though the doctors said he would die. The bullet severed part of his brain and they said he would never walk or talk, but I prayed the prayer of faith and six months later he came to youth group walking and talking!

But I have also prayed in faith for people to live and then watched them die.

Opening the Door to Blessing

I don't always know why. We may not have some answers this side of Heaven. But that doesn't shake my faith.

My job is to be in faith; God's job is to take care of the results. If I prayed in faith and don't get an answer, that's not my responsibility. I may not know why, but God is still God.

So how does faith work?

Jesus gave us a simple definition: *"Therefore I say to you, whatever things you ask when you pray, believe that you receive them, and you will have them"* (Mark 11:24 *NKJV*).

SO HOW DOES

FAITH WORK?

Notice that He said we believe we receive before we have it.

Our natural tendency is to say we believe that we receive when we have it—but that is a fact. That is not faith.

Faith believes we have it before we hold it in our hands.

How did you get saved? By faith.

The Bible tells us *"that if you confess with your mouth the Lord Jesus and believe in your heart that God has raised Him from the dead, you will be saved. For with the heart one believes unto righteousness, and with the mouth confession is made unto salvation"* (Romans 10:9-10 *NKJV*).

Faith believes in your heart and speaks with your mouth. That's how you got saved, and that's how you'll get the answers to your prayers.

God, What's Taking So Long?

How do you know you are in faith? The words coming out of your mouth reveal what you believe in your heart!

Some people have more faith in the enemy's power to curse them than God's power to bless them. They are accepting his curse when their words agree with the negative things the enemy wants to bring into their lives. Proverbs 18:21 says, "Life and death are in the power of the tongue!" They are signing for his packages with their words.

A lot of us aren't seeing the answer to our prayers because we're not in faith.

"But let him ask in faith, with no doubting, for he who doubts is like a wave of the sea driven and tossed by the wind. For let not that man suppose that he will receive anything from the Lord; he is a double-minded man, unstable in all his ways" (James 1:6-8 *NKJV*).

When we pray in faith, God answers—the answer to our prayer is en route to us. God has sent his delivery angel with our answer!

But if we start to doubt and speak negative words of unbelief, the delivery person turns around and heads back.

Then, if we get back in faith, the delivery person turns around again and starts coming toward us.

Before long, we doubt again, and get back to faith again—back and forth we go, back and forth the delivery person goes.

That sort of double-minded faith puts our answer in a holding pattern. To get answers to your prayers, get in faith with your words and stay in faith!

Discussion Questions

1. Does God promise to answer every prayer of every person? Are there any conditions involved?

2. Why does our praying show us our level of faith and reveal what we really believe about God?

3. What is the difference between a prayer request prayed "in hope" and a prayer request prayed "in faith"?

4. How does faith work? What are the steps involved when we pray in faith? Why are our prayers hindered when our prayers resemble a "double-minded delivery person"?

CHAPTER SIX

How Prayer Works

The process of prayer works much like the procedure in a courtroom. Now if you've had a bad experience in a courtroom, please try to stay with me—this is actually a good thing, and it's in your favor! Let's set the stage for how prayer works with a look at the heavenly courtroom.

The Judge

The Bible says that "God is the Judge; He puts down one, and exalts another" (Psalm 75:7 *NKJV*). He is "the Judge of all" (Hebrew 12:23 *NKJV*).

When we pray, we are presenting our requests to God, who is the righteous judge of all the earth.

Now if you're like me, this is what happens when we pray: I start asking God for something, but what comes to my mind is all the things I have done wrong. After all, I am standing before a righteous judge, and I'm suddenly very aware of why I am not worthy for God to answer my prayer.

MANY PEOPLE HAVE GIVEN UP ON PRAYER BECAUSE EVERY TIME THEY TRY TO COME INTO GOD'S PRESENCE THEY START THINKING ABOUT HOW MESSED UP THEY ARE.

Does this ever happen to you? Many people have given up on prayer because every time they try to come into God's presence they start thinking about how messed up they are.

Some of us are reluctant to pray because we feel that God expects us to have our life completely together before He will listen to us. But that would be like a doctor telling a patient they can't have medicine until they are better. Prayer is what helps us get our life together.

God isn't the one condemning us when we blow it. That's somebody else's job. So who else is in the courtroom? That's right—the prosecutor.

The Prosecutor

Satan is the one who accuses you of your sins and wants to condemn you with a guilty sentence. He is the one who prosecutes your mind for all you have done wrong. The Bible calls him "the accuser of our brethren" (Revelation 12:10 *NKJV*).

Satan is the one who presents all the evidence against you to show that you are not worthy of God answering you.

But there is good news, really good news—we have the top Defense Attorney in the universe on our side!

The Defense Attorney

"My little children, these things I write to you, so that you may not sin. And if anyone sins, we have an Advocate with the Father, Jesus Christ the righteous" (1 John 2:1 *NKJV*). "Advocate" means "a pleader in a court of law." Jesus stands beside us in the courtroom as our defense attorney.

God is "the Judge of all," the Bible says, but Jesus is "the Mediator of the new covenant" (Hebrews 12:22-24 *NKJV*). "Mediator" means "go-between." When we come to God the Father to present our requests, we have our Defense Attorney, Jesus, to represent us.

The Evidence

The trial begins when you go to God in prayer.

The prosecutor, Satan, jumps in and accuses you of crimes against God's laws and he presents his evidence against you.

Unfortunately, he built his case on solid facts. You have blown it! You have broken God's laws. If it weren't true you

wouldn't feel bad. Satan brings his charges against you—
"Lying! Lust! Anger!"—and for proof he simply replays the
truth in your mind. We have all fallen short of God's stan-
dards. We have all been guilty of sin since the fall of Adam
and Eve.

After creating Heaven and earth, God created Adam
and Eve and placed them in the Garden of Eden.

The first thing God said to Adam was, "Don't."

"Don't what?" Adam asked.

God said, "Don't eat the forbidden fruit."

"Forbidden fruit? We've got forbidden fruit? Hey, Eve!
We've got forbidden fruit!"

Eve says, "No way!"

Adam says, "Yes way!"

"Don't eat that fruit," God said.

"Why not?"

"Because I am your Father and I said so!"

Perhaps for a moment God wondered why He hadn't
stopped after He made elephants. If you're a parent, this
should be encouraging for you if you ever feel frustrated
while raising your children. Even God the Father had diffi-
culty with the first kids He created.

It wasn't long before God saw his kids taking an
apple break.

"Didn't I tell you not to eat the fruit?"

"Uh huh," Adam said.

"Then why did you?"

"I dunno," Adam said.

"I dunno," Eve said.

"She started it!" Adam said.

"Did not!"

"Did too!"

"Did not!"

"I've had it with the two of you," God said. "I told you there would be consequences..."

Thus, the pattern of sin was set and it has never been changed. But it's not true that God's punishment for Adam and Eve was giving them children of their own.

The Cross-Examination

After Satan brings his accusations, Jesus begins His cross-examination by bringing His own evidence.

"And you, being dead in your trespasses...He has made alive together with Him, having forgiven you all trespasses, having wiped out the handwriting of requirements that was against us,

which was contrary to us. And He has taken it out of the way, having nailed it to the cross" (Colossians 2:13-14 *NKJV*).

Jesus took the crimes and the written citations against us and He nailed our "rap sheet" to the cross. When He did that, He wiped out all the evidence against us!

Jesus sums up His case in two words: "What evidence?" Then He shows God the Judge the holes in His hands and feet, and says, "Put those accusations in the shredder!" Jesus Himself sits in the mercy seat for us to declare our innocence because of His sacrifice for us.

THERE MAY HAVE BEEN PEOPLE IN YOUR LIFE WHO HAVE TOLD YOU WHY YOU CAN'T AND WHY YOU WON'T CHANGE, AND WHY YOU ARE NOT GOOD ENOUGH, BUT THEIR VOTE MEANS NOTHING BEFORE GOD.

The Jury

You may notice the absence of something familiar—in many courtrooms there is a jury, only in Heaven there isn't one. Your fate and your future are not in the hands of other people!

There may have been people in your life who have told you why you can't and why you won't change, and why you are not good enough, but their vote means nothing before God. Their voice is stricken from the heavenly courtroom!

Closing Arguments

After the prosecutor makes his case, and our Defense Attorney makes His case, it's time for the closing arguments.

This is where many people blow it. Rather than simply agreeing with Jesus their Advocate, they agree with their accuser! They get up and change seats. Instead of sitting next to Jesus at the defense table, they go sit beside Satan. When it's their turn to testify, they start to agree with the prosecutor: "You are right! I am not worthy! I am messed up! Why would God ever listen to me?"

Then they give up in their prayers and walk away feeling worse than before they prayed.

They're like the elderly man who went to visit the doctor. "Doc," he says, "I am so stricken. I have chest pains, headaches, back pains, nausea, arthritis, constipation, stomach cramps, earaches, burning in the eyes, congested lungs."

"Wow," replied the doctor. "Those are some serious symptoms. Is there anything you don't have?" The man answered, "Teeth."

We need to stop looking at the negative. When you're praying and you hear the accusations against you, there's only one way to close the case—agree with your Advocate!

"Seeing then that we have a great High Priest who has passed through the heavens, Jesus the Son of God, let us hold fast our confession" (Hebrews 4:14 NKJV).

The word "confession" in the New Testament can also be translated "profession," which means "to speak the same thing or to be in agreement."

We are to agree with Jesus when He says that through His sacrifice for our sins, we are completely forgiven and washed in His blood—*"for the accuser of our brethren, who accused them before our God day and night, has been cast down. And they overcame him by the blood of the Lamb and by the word of their testimony"* (Revelation 12:10-11 *NKJV*).

We overcome feelings of guilt and condemnation by the blood of Jesus and by the word of our testimony! When we testify, we should speak the same thing as Christ. And He says we are forgiven—and that is what we say, too!

Our Legal Rights

In the same way that we are free in America because of the brave men and women who paid the price of their blood, we are free because Jesus paid the price of His blood for our freedom. This is where many of us stop short. We believe Jesus died for our forgiveness, but fail to understand that He died to give us our freedom and our legal (covenant) rights.

We saw that Jesus is "the Mediator of the new covenant" (Hebrews 12:22-24)—but what is this new covenant?

In today's terms, a "covenant" is a legal contract. The Bible contains the terms of our legal rights as believers. As

you may know, the Bible is divided into two main parts—
the Old Testament and New Testament. As Christians, we
live under the New Testament. A "testament" is the same
thing as in "Last Will and Testament." God has provided us
with a legal will and testament that lists what we have inher-
ited as His children. A will is activated upon the death of
the testator, and we have come into our inheritance in the
family of God.

Our legal rights were activated by Jesus's death, and now
we are *"giving thanks to the Father who has qualified us to be
partakers of the inheritance of the saints in the light. He has delivered us from the power of darkness and conveyed us into the kingdom
of the Son of His love, in whom we have redemption through His
blood, the forgiveness of sins"* (Colossians 1:12-14 *NKJV*).

Redemption

The Bible portrays us as being on the auction block in
the slave market of sin. Slave auctions are among the most
degrading and inhuman places in human history. Slaves
would have their mouths forced open and their teeth
inspected. They were often disrobed. They were kicked
and punched by the ruthless and heartless slave traders.

As slaves of sin, we were under a cruel and heartless
taskmaster, who kicked and abused and humiliated us. But
Jesus delivered us from Satan—He rescued us and
redeemed us by paying the full price for our freedom, and

He carried us away to become part of His family. We are no longer under the rule of Satan and his cruelty.

JESUS HAS
REDEEMED US
FROM EVERYTHING
SATAN HAD USED
TO HARM US.

Now, in addition to being the proof of purchase of our redemption, the Bible is also the legal contract of our family rights! Our purchase price has been paid in full! Jesus has redeemed us from everything Satan had used to harm us. We aren't just forgiven—we are free!

The Appeal Process

When someone appeals a case to a judge, they are basically asking the judge to review the status of their case and uphold their legal rights. Prayer is an appeal to God—the righteous Judge, and our Father—to uphold our legal right to our spiritual inheritance.

"Now this is the confidence that we have in Him, that if we ask anything according to His will, He hears us. And if we know that He hears us, whatever we ask, we know that we have the petitions that we have asked of Him" (1 John 5:14-15 NKJV).

We can have confidence that God will answer our prayers. The only condition is that anything we ask be according to His will.

What is His will? His Word is His will!

So when we pray the Word of God, we are praying the will of God! If I am praying the will of God, He grants what I pray for. So we need to know the Word so we know what to pray.

We see in the Word that we have the legal right to be healthy—1 Peter 2:24.

We see in the Word that we have the legal right to have all our needs met—Philippians 4:19.

We see in the Word that we have the legal right to peace of mind—John 14:27.

We see in the Word that we have the legal right to divine wisdom—James 1:5.

So we pray the Word, the Word is God's will, God hears our prayers and we have the answer!

The Thief

Have you noticed that even though you live in America and you have clear constitutional rights, there are some people who attempt to violate your rights?

We have the right to peace in our homes, but try telling that to my ex-neighbor with the teenage son who played his drums after midnight.

We have the right to own property, but there are robbers and thieves who try to steal from us.

God, What's Taking So Long?

We have the right to live, but there are people who kill others and take that right away.

As you can imagine, Satan tries to do the same thing. As your former slave owner, he's angry and still wants to be your master. He isn't content to let you live under the blessing of God, so he tries to violate your legal covenant rights.

MANY PEOPLE WRONGLY BELIEVE THAT GOD CAUSES BAD THINGS TO HAPPEN AND THAT HE'S DOING THESE THINGS TO TEACH US A LESSON.

Satan wants to steal the blessings God has given you. Jesus said, *"The thief does not come except to steal, and to kill, and to destroy"* (John 10:10 *NKJV*). He wants you to be sick, to be sad, to be mad and not glad. He wants you poor, broke and busted!

Many people wrongly believe that God causes bad things to happen and that He's doing these things to teach us a lesson. Insurance companies have a clause called the "Act of God" clause—they say God is responsible for tornados and natural disasters. Ridiculous!

Sometimes at funerals, you'll even hear preachers make ignorant statements like, "God took little Sissy home because He needed another flower for His rose garden." What? God doesn't need little Sissy in Heaven more than her mom and dad need her in their lives. God enjoyed seeing little Sissy here on earth—He didn't need to take her home. Satan is the one who kills, steals, and destroys.

Stop blaming God and start putting the blame on the creep who used to be your old slave master!

Jesus is the exact representation of the Father (Hebrews 1:1-4). He said He only did what He saw the Father doing (John 5:19). We can look at Jesus' life on earth and see what God is like. *"The thief does not come except to steal, and to kill, and to destroy,"* Jesus said. *"I have come that they may have life, and that they may have it more abundantly"* (John 10:10 *NKJV*).

If sickness is something God puts on people to teach them, then Jesus would have given people sickness. Instead, He healed them.

Jesus never caused a storm, but He did say, "Peace, be still" to a storm.

Jesus never took a person's livelihood away, but he did take bread and fish and multiplied it to feed thousands of people until they were too full to eat anymore.

Jesus didn't die to redeem us from the slave market of sin so the devil could continue to abuse us. Jesus said if the Son sets you free, you will be free indeed! (John 8:36).

The Rebuttal

Satan the accuser presents his evidence that you still belong to him. He claims to have the right to abuse you with sickness.

"Here is the doctor's report," he asserts. "Just listen to that cough!"

He holds up more evidence to claim he has the right to keep you poor.

He holds up all your bills, he holds up your small pay stub—and then he rests his case.

The Surrebuttal

But this new evidence brought by the accuser is all circumstantial—and circumstantial evidence does not prove a fact, it merely assumes that a fact exists.

Direct evidence is always stronger than circumstantial evidence in a court of law. The Word of God, for example, is direct evidence—and so is the testimony of Jesus when He takes the stand as our witness. Jesus took the evidence against us and He nailed it to the cross. He will testify under direct examination that our debt is paid in full, that we are redeemed from every thing that the thief has against us, and that the devil has no right to our lives any more!

Closing Arguments

We believe the direct evidence of God's Word is above any circumstantial evidence. We don't get up and walk over to sit with our accuser.

How Prayer Works

"Seeing then that we have a great High Priest who has passed through the heavens, Jesus the Son of God, let us hold fast our confession" (Hebrews 4:14 *NKJV*).

Therefore, we speak the same thing God says!

We say to that thief, "Stop in the name of Jesus! You have no power over me any more. I am redeemed from poverty, lack, fear, depression, oppression, congestion—I am free and free indeed!"

I agree with God!

Discussion Questions

1. According to the courtroom analogy used in this chapter, how is the "direct evidence" of God's Word above all "circumstantial evidence"?

2. How does it benefit the devil when you agree with him about your sins and weaknesses?

3. Do you ever find yourself praying more confidently on some occasions and praying more reluctantly on others? Why do you suppose that is?

4. Again, using the courtroom analogy, what defense does Jesus offer in response to the prosecutor's charges?

Prerequisites to Prayer

Many people don't realize that God doesn't give us carte blanche on prayer. There are certain prerequisites for having your prayers answered.

1. In Forgiveness

Next to faith, forgiveness is the most important component to answered prayer.

"Therefore I say to you, whatever things you ask when you pray, believe that you receive them, and you will have them. 'And whenever you stand praying, if you have anything against anyone, forgive him that your Father in heaven may also forgive you your trespasses. But if you do not forgive, neither will your Father in heaven forgive your trespasses" (Mark 11:24-26 NKJV).

Over and over, when Jesus talked about prayer, He talked about forgiveness. Nothing will kill your prayers faster than resentment and unforgiveness. When you hold a grudge, when you nurse an ill feeling, when you allow bitterness to grow in your life, your prayers are canceled. Maybe the reason you're not getting an answer to your prayer is because you're holding a grudge against somebody.

"Husbands, likewise, dwell with them with understanding, giving honor to the wife, as to the weaker vessel, and as being heirs together of the grace of life, that your prayers may not be hindered" (1 Peter 3:7 *NKJV*).

IF YOU'RE NOT TREATING YOUR WIFE LIKE FINE CHINA, YOU MAY NOT BE RECEIVING THE ANSWERS TO YOUR PRAYERS.

Disharmony in the home blocks our prayers. If you're not treating your wife like fine china, you may not be receiving the answers to your prayers. You've probably discovered by now that the easiest place to get offended and bitter is at home. We need to forgive each other and work out our differences.

Jesus illustrated the importance of forgiveness in a parable.

"Therefore the kingdom of heaven is like a certain king who wanted to settle accounts with his servants. And when he had begun to settle accounts, one was brought to him who owed him ten thousand talents. But as he was not able to pay, his master commanded that he be sold, with his wife and children and all that he had, and that payment be made" (Matthew 18:23-25 *NJKV*).

This man owed the king a sum of 10,000 talents. One talent was equivalent to 10,000 denarii, and a denarius was the wage paid for one day's work. So a man would have to work 250 days a year for 40 years to earn one talent (figuring five days a week with two weeks annual vacation). So that means a man would work most of his life to earn *one* talent—and this man owed 10,000 talents!

So to put this in modern terms, if this man was earning $30,000 a year, his debt would be around $300 million dollars. If he held an executive position that paid $100,000 a year, his debt would be close to $1 billion dollars. And in either case, if this man was in prison, how was he going to make the money to repay the debt?

There was no hope for this man.

"The servant therefore fell down before him, saying, 'Master, have patience with me, and I will pay you all.' Then the master of that servant was moved with compassion, released him, and forgave him the debt" (Matthew 18:26-27 *NKJV*).

He asked for mercy—and the master forgave him the debt.

This was not an extension of repayment terms. He owed a debt equivalent to what he could earn over 10,000 lifetimes—and that doesn't even include the interest—but the master cancelled the bill! Imagine you were unable to pay your home mortgage and they cancelled it. This man could have never repaid that debt, but the king had mercy.

IMAGINE YOU WERE UNABLE TO PAY YOUR HOME MORTGAGE AND THEY CANCELLED IT.

However, there's more to this story.

"But that servant went out and found one of his fellow servants who owed him a hundred denarii; and he laid hands on him and took him by the throat, saying, 'Pay me what you owe!'" (Matthew 18:28 *NKJV*).

Later, when he found a man that owed him 100 denarii, he got up in his grill.

Don't you think the man should have been full of forgiveness because he had just been forgiven? True, the fellow servant owed him a lot of money—since a denarius was a day's wage, this was close to four months' salary, which would mean, if the man was making $30,000 a year, he owed him $10,000. But what is that compared to the $300 million to $1 billion he had owed the king?

"So his fellow servant fell down at his feet and begged him, saying, 'Have patience with me, and I will pay you all.' And he would not, but went and threw him into prison till he should pay the debt. So when his fellow servants saw what had been done, they were very grieved, and came and told their master all that had been done. Then his master, after he had called him, said to him, 'You wicked servant! I forgave you all that debt because you begged me. Should you not also have had compassion on your fellow servant, just as I had pity on you?' And his master was angry, and delivered him to the torturers until he should pay all that was due to him. So My heavenly Father also will do to you if each of you, from his heart, does not forgive his brother his trespasses" (Matthew 18:29-35 *NKJV*).

No matter how big the offense someone has toward you, it is mere pennies in comparison to what God has forgiven you.

God has forgiven us, and we must choose to forgive others.

"Therefore, as the elect of God, holy and beloved, put on...longsuffering; bearing with one another, and forgiving one another, if anyone has a complaint against another; even as Christ forgave you, so you also must do" (Colossians 3:12-13 *NKJV*).

> NO MATTER HOW BIG THE OFFENSE SOMEONE HAS TOWARD YOU, IT IS MERE PENNIES IN COMPARISON TO WHAT GOD HAS FORGIVEN YOU.

The Bible tells us to clothe ourselves in longsuffering. Longsuffering doesn't sound like something we're going to like, does it?

But longsuffering is our spiritual garment.

What happens if you don't put on your clothes before you go work? You get there naked.

In the same way, when we don't forgive, we are naked— the weaknesses we have been covering up are exposed to the world. I don't know about you, but I find myself feeling sorry for people when I see them filled with bitterness and unforgiveness.

So how do we forgive someone when we don't feel like it?

God, What's Taking So Long?

First, I focus on how God has forgiven me over and over and over again.

Second, it becomes much easier for me to forgive those who have sinned against me when I remember how many times I have needed others to forgive me.

You may be thinking, "I will forgive them when they ask for it." But the sad truth is you may be waiting a long time—you may wait your whole lifetime and never hear those words.

We need to remember that someone else's irresponsibility never releases us from our responsibility. We have to do the right thing—whether they do or not.

Third, we need to keep in mind that forgiveness is not minimizing the seriousness of the offense. It's not saying, "This is not a big deal. It's okay; it didn't really hurt me."

THE DEPTH OF TRUE FORGIVENESS IS FOUND IN THE DEPTH OF THE PAIN.

That is not true forgiveness. The depth of true forgiveness is found in the depth of the pain. When we minimize the hurt we are feeling, we are minimizing the forgiveness required. The depth of our sin reveals the height of God's love.

So it's okay to admit how much the offense hurt. We just choose to forgive.

We have to understand that forgiveness doesn't mean there won't still be some pain. Some offenses against us can hurt very deeply.

Prerequisites to Prayer

I can forgive someone and still have pain. Forgiveness means I am giving up my right to get even. But it may take a long time for the pain to go away. Some injuries may even leave scars that last a lifetime. But forgiveness keeps the wounds in our heart from getting infected and will allow them to heal properly.

Finally, forgiveness doesn't mean we automatically resume trusting the person who sinned against us. Forgiveness is instant, but trust is built over a period of time. Some offenses may require a long time of rebuilding trust. Sometimes the offender will have to work hard for a season to prove they are responsible and trustworthy before certain privileges are restored.

One way you can tell if you have forgiven someone is if you can pray for that person. And I don't mean pray that God will smite them.

Jesus is our example of praying for those who hurt Him. Wouldn't you agree that if anyone had cause for unforgiveness it was Jesus? He only did good to people—He fed the hungry, He opened the eyes of the blind, He taught life changing lessons—yet He was betrayed.

But on the cross He prayed, "Father, forgive them, for they do not know what they do" (Luke 23:28 NKJV).

It's hard to hate someone when you're praying for him or her. When you pray for them you begin to see them through God's eyes.

God, What's Taking So Long?

There have been times someone has hurt me and I took it personally. It made me feel like something was wrong with me. Their harsh words became weights on my soul. But when I prayed for them I began to get God's perspective. I saw that they didn't know what they were doing. I began to feel compassion for them. I realized that hurting people hurt people!

We have truly forgiven someone when we can pray that God will bless that person.

"Beloved, do not avenge yourselves, but rather give place to wrath; for it is written, 'Vengeance is Mine, I will repay,' says the Lord. Therefore 'If your enemy is hungry, feed him; If he is thirsty, give him a drink; For in so doing you will heap coals of fire on his head.' Do not be overcome by evil, but overcome evil with good" (Romans 12:19-21 *NKJV*).

"Wait a minute!" you may be thinking. "That isn't fair!"

You're probably right. They hurt you and that certainly wasn't fair to you and it certainly wouldn't be fair if they got off the hook. The only fair thing is that they should get what they deserve.

WE WANT LIFE TO BE FAIR FOR US BUT WE REALLY DON'T WANT GOD TO BE FAIR WITH US.

But first let me ask you a question: "Do you want God to be fair with you and give you what you deserve?"

We are talking about being fair, right? Was it fair for Jesus to forgive everything you've ever done wrong and let you go free? Was it fair that He had to die on the cross for your sins? We want life to be fair for us but we really don't want God to be fair with us.

One of the main reasons we don't want to forgive is because we want to take vengeance in our own hands. It's a form of revenge—"You owe me! I am going to make you pay for what you did to me!"

But think about that for a moment. How does our unforgiveness hurt them? Does it really hurt them in any way?

Who does it really hurt?

It hurts us!

"And his master was angry, and delivered him to the torturers until he should pay all that was due to him. So My heavenly Father also will do to you if each of you, from his heart, does not forgive his brother his trespasses" (Matthew 18:34-35 *NKJV*).

People who don't forgive live in torment. They rehearse the offense over and over in their minds. They fret about it and lose sleep over it. In the end, they become the prisoners!

So instead of being overcome by evil, we need to overcome evil with good. We need to find ways to bless those who have offended us. What good thing can you do for those who have hurt you? My wife and I have even bought gifts for some people who have hurt us.

Did they deserve it? That's beside the point. Instead, we should ask, "What is the foundation of Christianity?"

God forgave us the debt we did deserve and gave us what we didn't deserve. He forgave us. And we should do the same for others. When we forgive others we are acting like our heavenly Father.

Look at the word *forgiveness* for a moment. *For-give-ness.* Do you see the word in the middle? There is no forgiveness without the word "give." Forgiveness involves giving in some way to someone who doesn't deserve it. Isn't that what God does every day for each one of us?

2. In Unselfishness

How many prayers go unanswered because they are completely selfish? Next time you pray, ask yourself, "Why am I asking God for this? Is it entirely about me?"

The Bible warns us that *"you do not have because you do not ask. You ask and do not receive, because you ask amiss, that you may spend it on your pleasures"* (James 4:2-3 *NKJV*).

If you are praying for health are you going to use it to serve God, to go to church, to get involved in a ministry and do something for others? Or are you praying for health so you can do things that will take you out of church, away from God and away from serving people?

If you are praying for money, what are you going to use it for? Is it all for you? Or are you praying, "God bless me so I can be a blessing to others"?

Are you praying for your spouse so that your life will be more convenient and so you feel better, or are you praying out of a genuine concern that your spouse will experience God's best?

Looking back over my life, I can recall many unanswered prayers because of this issue right here—my prayers were all about me and nobody else.

3. In God's Will

When we pray we need to pray in line with God's will.

"Now this is the confidence that we have in Him, that if we ask anything according to His will, He hears us. And if we know that He hears us, whatever we ask, we know that we have the petitions that we have asked of Him" (1 John 5:14-15 *NKJV*).

When we pray for something according to God's will, then we are confident in prayer because we know He's going to answer. Many of our prayers go unanswered because they are not His will. Of course, sometimes this is a good thing. When I was single I would sometimes pray, "Lord, let *her* be the one." I am glad God didn't answer any of those prayers. Years later I found God's will for my wife, and His will was better for me than my will.

THERE ARE OVER 10,000 PROMISES IN GOD'S WORD. WHEN WE PRAY FOR ANY OF THOSE PROMISES, WE ARE PRAYING THE WILL OF GOD.

How do I know the will of God? God's Word is His will. There are over 10,000 promises in His Word. When we pray for any of those promises, we are praying the will of God.

4. In Faith

Have you ever thought you were following God—and then you encountered some problems? Did you begin to feel alone and even question if you had really heard His voice? The disciples faced that situation one night when Jesus told them to get into a boat and cross the sea.

THEY HAD OBEYED JESUS, AND IT HAD LANDED THEM IN THE MIDDLE OF A STORM.

"But the boat was now in the middle of the sea, tossed by the waves, for the wind was contrary" (Matthew 14:24 *NKJV*).

They had obeyed Jesus, and it had landed them in the middle of a storm!

"Now in the fourth watch of the night Jesus went to them, walking on the sea. And when the disciples saw Him walking on the sea, they were troubled, saying, 'It is a ghost!' And they cried out for fear. But immediately Jesus spoke to them, saying, 'Be of good cheer! It is I; do not be afraid'" (Matthew 14:25-27 *NKJV*).

Jesus was walking on their problem. The thing we fear, Jesus eats for breakfast.

Notice that the first thing Jesus says to them in the midst of the storm is, "Cheer up! I am here." He didn't say, "What's wrong with you guys? You worthless, no good, messed up people with no faith!"

"And Peter answered Him and said, 'Lord, if it is You, command me to come to You on the water.' So He said, 'Come.' And when Peter had come down out of the boat, he walked on the water to go to Jesus. But when he saw that the wind was boisterous, he was afraid; and beginning to sink he cried out, saying, 'Lord, save me!'" (Matthew 14:28-30 NKJV).

Peter called to Jesus and asked if he could join Him walking on the water. Jesus invited him out, so Peter got out of the boat and started to walk—but then the winds and waters frightened him and he began to sink.

It's the same for us. When we get our eyes off Jesus and on our problems we begin to sink. What do winds and waves matter in regard to walking on the water? Peter wasn't walking on the water—he was walking on the words of Jesus. He didn't get far that night, but now let's jump years ahead to another night.

> PETER WASN'T WALKING ON THE WATER—HE WAS WALKING ON THE WORDS OF JESUS.

On this evening we find Peter in prison, in chains between two guards, scheduled for a public trial and execution. How well would you sleep the night before your execution? How well do you sleep now when faced with problems at work, at home, or with your money?

Peter was sound asleep.

"Now behold, an angel of the Lord stood by him, and a light shone in the prison; and he struck Peter on the side and raised him up, saying, 'Arise quickly!' And his chains fell off his hands" (Acts 12:7 NKJV).

Peter may have started out with little faith, and found himself sinking into the water, but over time he grew. He took steps. Here we see him peacefully sleeping the night before his impending execution. He had gotten to the point where he had confidence in God's Word.

5. In Agreement

IF SOMEONE SAYS THEY ARE 100% IN AGREEMENT ON EVERY LITTLE DETAIL WITH ANOTHER PERSON, THEN SOMEONE ISN'T BEING HONEST.

"Can two walk together, unless they are agreed?" (Amos 3:3 NKJV). When we don't agree with another person, it is hard to have a relationship.

Now let me qualify this statement for a moment. This doesn't mean we run out and cut off every relationship where we have some disagreement. I don't think there is anyone who I have ever agreed with 100%. If someone says they are 100% in agreement on every little detail with another person, then someone isn't being honest.

Prerequisites to Prayer

Most of the disagreements I have had with people aren't major enough to cut off that relationship, but some have been. Most of the time I choose to respect their right to have a wrong opinion. We agree to disagree, and, like Steven Covey says, we "major on the majors and minor on the minors."

The exception to this rule is with God. His opinion is 100% right 100% of the time. It is my responsibility to agree with Him. When I choose to disagree with Him, it affects my ability to walk with Him. This includes being in disagreement with His Word—many people are struggling in some area of their life because the words coming out of their mouths are not in agreement with God's Word.

Discussion Questions

1. How can we forgive someone who does not seem to feel sorry about hurting us in the past and may even choose to hurt us in the future?

2. How can you know when you've truly forgiven someone?

3. If God does not answer "selfish" prayers, what is the difference between a "selfish" prayer and an "unselfish" prayer? Is there a way we can pray for ourselves—for our finances, for our families, for our health—in an "unselfish" manner?

4. How can we know that our prayer requests are in line with God's will?

CHAPTER EIGHT

Establishing Our Covenant

When we pray, what gives us the right to approach God in prayer? How do we know He is going to listen? And how do we know He is going to answer our prayers?

It comes down to one thing: God's covenant with us through Jesus.

Our covenant is the foundation for everything in our walk with God. Let's look at the seven ways that covenants were expressed in the Bible to help us better understand the covenant relationship we have with God today.

1. Exchange Coats

In ancient times, people making a covenant would exchange their coats or robes. The cloak represented the person, their authority, and ownership of their properties and possessions.

OUR COVENANT IS

THE FOUNDATION

FOR EVERYTHING

IN OUR WALK

WITH GOD.

"Then Jonathan and David made a covenant...and Jonathan took off the robe that was on him and gave it to David with his armor, even to his sword and his bow and his belt" (1 Samuel 18:3-4 *NKJV*).

By giving David his robe, Jonathan was symbolically giving his identity to him in covenant. Jonathan was King Saul's son and wore a royal robe of authority. David was a shepherd. Jonathan was exchanging his royal robe for David's plain clothing.

In the same way, Christ exchanged His royal robe of righteousness for our filthy rags.

Isaiah said our righteousness is as filthy rags before God (Isaiah 64:6), but Jesus took our filthy rags to the cross and gave us His righteousness. *"For He made Him who knew no sin to be sin for us, that we might become the righteousness of God in Him"* (2 Corinthians 5:21 *NKJV*).

In our covenant with God, He has given us His royal robe of righteousness. Many Christians are trying to become righteous because they don't realize they are already righteous. So they're doing good works to become righteous, rather than doing good works because they already are righteous—and that's a big difference!

Now that God has said we are already righteous through Jesus, we just need to be renewed in our minds and put on the righteousness of Christ.

How do we do this? The Bible says we *"put on the Lord Jesus Christ"* (Romans 13:14 *NKJV*) when we *"put on the new man which was created according to God, in true righteousness and holiness"* (Ephesians 4:24 *NKJV*). In simple terms, that means we live on the outside what we have become on the inside.

One practical way to help us put on our righteousness in Christ is water baptism. *"For as many of you as were baptized into Christ have put on Christ"* (Galatians 3:29 *NKJV*). Baptism is an outward sign of an inward work.

We need to start agreeing with what God says we are. We live up to what we believe we are. If we think we are losers, then we will act like losers. If we see ourselves as the righteousness of God, we live righteously.

2. Exchange Belts

In ancient times, a belt held weapons in place and symbolized power. When two warriors exchanged belts, they were pledging their strength, support, protection and to fight for one another.

"The Lord will cause your enemies who rise against you to be defeated before your face; they shall come out against you one way and flee before you seven ways" (Deuteronomy 28:7 *NKJV*).

This is why a seventeen-year-old shepherd named David could kill a nine-foot giant wearing more than 300 pounds of armor. David wasn't operating out of his intellect; he was speaking out of a faith that came from his understanding of his covenant with God.

The giants in your life are not yours to face alone—your enemies are now God's enemies. He fights your battles. Jesus came to defeat our adversary the devil. *"And they overcame him by the blood of the Lamb and by the word of their testimony, and they did not love their lives to the death"* (Revelation 12:11 *NKJV*).

When we speak the words of God, He fulfills His covenant to fight our battles. Life and death are in the power of the tongue. How careful are you with your words?

A Jewish man went to his rabbi and said he needed advice on how to stop gossiping. The wise rabbi said, "Go home, get your pillow and punch it full of holes. Let the feathers fly in the wind. Then come back to me."

The man did as the rabbi said and then went back to the rabbi.

"Excellent," the rabbi said. "Now go back and gather all the feathers and put them back in the pillow."

"But that's impossible!" the man said. "The feathers have flown everywhere."

The rabbi nodded. "Yes," he said.

What words are you scattering over your life—death and defeat, or life and victory? Are you agreeing with God's Word, or with the enemy?

3. Cut a Covenant

In ancient times, the act of making a covenant was called "cutting a covenant" because the two individuals involved would kill an animal and split it down the middle, and then would walk between the pieces of flesh. This demonstrated their willingness to give up the rights to their own lives and begin a new walk with their covenant partner unto death.

We see this when God established His covenant with Abraham.

"So He said to him, 'Bring Me a three-year-old heifer, a three-year-old female goat, a three-year-old ram, a turtledove, and a young pigeon.' Then he brought all these to Him and cut them in two, down the middle, and placed each piece opposite the other" (Genesis 15:9-10 *NKJV*).

There are equal covenants and unequal ones. God's covenant with Abraham was unequal. God knew Abraham couldn't fully live up to his end of the agreement so He Himself cut the covenant. He kept the agreement for Abraham.

"And it came to pass, when the sun went down and it was dark, that behold, there appeared a smoking oven and a burning torch that passed between those pieces. On the same day the Lord made a covenant with Abram" (Genesis 15:17-18 *NKJV*).

We are saved not by works but by grace. We are not able to be perfect like God, so Jesus fulfilled the covenant agreement for us. He cut a covenant for us.

4. Exchange Names

In ancient times, the two individuals cutting a covenant would exchange names as a means of identifying with one another. This was often represented by a hyphen between the old name and the new name. This change of names indicated that the two families had now become one new family.

We have been given a new name. We are now called "Christians"—which identifies us as being "Christ ones" and "ones belonging to Christ."

We have been given the name of Christ—to our immediate benefit:

"And whatever you ask in My name, that I will do, that the Father may be glorified in the Son. If you ask anything in My name, I will do it" (John 14:13-14 NKJV).

"And in that day you will ask Me nothing. Most assuredly, I say to you, whatever you ask the Father in My name He will give you. Until now you have asked nothing in My name. Ask, and you will receive, that your joy may be full" (John 16:23-24 NKJV).

A great picture of our covenant with God can be seen in Little Orphan Annie. She was a poor orphan but then she won the heart of Daddy Warbucks, the billionaire. When he adopted her, she became a "Warbucks" and she was entitled to everything that went with her new family name. When we were spiritual orphans, God adopted us and we now carry His name, "Christian," and we have all the benefits that this name carries!

Too many Christians act like they are ashamed of their new name. We whisper, "I am a Christian," like we are carrying a disease. We should hold our heads high, proud to carry the name of Christ. I know I will never be ashamed of my faith—Jesus wasn't ashamed to die for me and I will never be ashamed to live for Him!

> JESUS WASN'T ASHAMED TO DIE FOR ME AND I WILL NEVER BE ASHAMED TO LIVE FOR HIM!

5. The Terms

In ancient times, after they cut the covenant, they would then give the terms of the covenant, pledging to commit their assets to one another and taking responsibility for the other's liabilities.

When Dr. Stanley was conducting his well-known search for Dr. Livingston in Africa, he was confronted by a powerful tribe that blocked his progress. His guide explained that if he wanted to proceed with his journey, he would have to cut a covenant with the chief of that tribe. Dr. Stanley agreed.

Before blood was shed, they had to exchange gifts. Dr. Stanley was not in good health and had brought a goat with him for its milk. When the chief said that he wanted the goat, it was a difficult decision for Dr. Stanley, but he gave him his goat.

As his gift in return, Dr. Stanley received a tall spear wrapped with copper. He later admitted that he was not very impressed. After all, what practical good would it be to him?

After the covenant was completed, Dr. Stanley continued on his journey.

But as they went along their way, they encountered some locals who noticed the spear and stopped to bow before Dr. Stanley. Then Dr. Stanley learned that the chief had given him the symbol of his own royal authority.

Stanley had been worried about losing a goat, but now he carried with him the authority to request anything he wanted—including the milk from a whole herd of goats!

God has made the terms of His covenant with us clear— He wants our ALL. Jesus said, *"You shall love the LORD your God with all your heart, with all your soul, with all your mind, and with all your strength"* (Mark 12:30 *NKJV*).

God refuses to be second. *"You shall have no other gods before Me"* (Exodus 20:3 *NKJV*).

All that we have becomes God's—but in exchange, all that He has is ours.

"But seek first the kingdom of God and His righteousness, and all these things shall be added to you" (Matthew 6:33 *NKJV*).

A person in a covenant could have and use whatever the other party owned. When God told Abraham to take his only son, Isaac, and offer him as a sacrifice, Abraham obeyed because of His covenant with God. Later, because Abraham was faithful to their covenant, God would give His only son, Jesus, on that same mountain.

When we give our tithe we are acknowledging our covenant and that all we have is God's. The good news is that He says all He has is ours. The terms of God's covenant with us are simple—we put Him first in our lives, and when we do, all His blessings are added to our lives.

6. The Meal

In ancient times, as well as in Eastern cultures throughout Asia and Africa, sharing a meal together is a sign of true fellowship. Often this involves reconciliation after a grievance has been committed. After both parties make a covenant to not take vengeance on each other, they sit down to a ceremonial meal.

We see this at the exodus from Egypt, as the people of Israel celebrated the Passover, and many still eat this meal to celebrate His faithfulness to them.

We see that Jesus included a meal in his story of the prodigal son. When the son comes home, his father arranges a feast to celebrate that his son has become part of the family again.

We see this after Jesus' resurrection, as we find Jesus cooking fish and serving breakfast to the disciples (John 21:9-19). Before the meal they talked about the break in their relationship. At Jesus's trial, Peter had denied him three times, but after the resurrection, three times Jesus asked Peter, "Do you love me?" They made peace and Jesus reinstated Peter as his disciple, and then they ate a meal together.

As Christians, when we receive communion it is a meal of reconciliation with God. It is a reminder that God will not take vengeance on us for our sins.

7. Plant A Tree

In ancient times, when people cut a covenant they would leave a memorial by planting a tree, which they sprinkled with the blood of the animal. This blood-sprinkled tree would be a lasting testimony to their sacred covenant relationship.

When Jesus paid the judgment of sin for us and cut a covenant with God on our behalf, He planted a memorial tree—the cross—and stained it with His own blood. The God who cannot change (Malachi 3:16) and who does not lie (Titus 1:2) has cut a covenant with you and me through the resurrection of His Son Jesus.

"Let us hold fast the confession of our hope without wavering, for He who promised is faithful" (Hebrews 10:23 NKJV).

"Confession" means to speak the same thing. What are we speaking in and over our lives? Are we agreeing with God so we can walk with Him? Or are we agreeing with the negative circumstances and walking in them? The choice is ours.

I choose life. I choose to agree with God's unbreakable covenant.

Sometimes I think we lose sight of how much God loves us, but we can see the depth of His love and mercy at the final Passover meal Jesus shared with His disciples.

"Then He took the cup, and gave thanks, and gave it to them, saying, 'Drink from it, all of you. For this is My blood of the new covenant, which is shed for many for the remission of sins'" (Matthew 26:27-28 *NKJV*).

SOMETIMES I THINK WE LOSE SIGHT OF HOW MUCH GOD LOVES US, BUT WE CAN SEE THE DEPTH OF HIS LOVE AND MERCY AT THE FINAL PASSOVER MEAL JESUS SHARED WITH HIS DISCIPLES.

Leonardo Da Vinci's famous painting of the last supper is a great painting, but the actual meal would have looked nothing like it. Instead, they'd have received communion at a table called a triclinium, which is low to the ground and U-shaped.

The seating arrangement had significance. The host sat in the middle of the left arm. On his right was his trusted friend and on his left was the seat of honor.

The close seat on his left arm would be the most important place, the seat beside it would be the next important place and the last place would be the least important— often the servant's seat. (This helps us understand Jesus' instructions to not take the seat of honor, but take the seat with least honor, doesn't it?)

At the last supper, Jesus would be in the host position, and John would have been on his right side—we know this because he leaned against Jesus to talk with Him. So who was on his left side, in the seat of honor?

"He answered and said, 'He who dipped his hand with Me in the dish will betray Me'" (Matthew 26:23 *NKJV*).

People shared a common dipping bowl with a person next to them. Jesus said that the person who would betray him was the person who dipped in the bowl with Him. We know it wasn't John who did this, so it must have been the person on His other side, in the seat of honor. And we know who it was that betrayed Him, so the person in the seat of honor who shared Jesus's dipping bowl must have been Judas.

Jesus had known that Judas would betray Him and yet He gave him the seat of honor. I would have put him at the end. Instead of giving him a seat, I would have kicked him in the seat.

Each one of us, like Judas, has betrayed Jesus with our sins. Yet, Jesus doesn't put us at the end of the table. He says, "I want you at my side. I still love you."

In spite of our betrayal, He still puts us in the seat of honor next to Him.

But at the table of your life, who has the seat of honor? Is it Jesus?

Or does Jesus sit at the end of your table with the servants? Some people see Jesus only as a servant, someone who is there to make them happy.

But in light of all Jesus has done for us, how can we not say, "God, I am sorry for putting You in any place less than the seat of honor in my life? Forgive me."

Happiness—real happiness—isn't "God, what can You do for me?" Instead, it's "God, what can I do for You?"

I am happy when I know that I have made Him happy. The real measure of my happiness can never be measured in this lifetime. That will come when I stand before God and hear Him say, "Well done, good and faithful servant. Enter into the joy of your Master."

I have true joy when I know I have brought Him joy with my life.

I HAVE TRUE JOY WHEN I KNOW I HAVE BROUGHT HIM JOY WITH MY LIFE.

Discussion Questions

1. In our covenant with God, everything that is His becomes ours, and everything that is ours becomes His. It's pretty obvious we benefit from this relationship— but what's in it for God?

2. We have been given a new name—Christian! Have you ever been reluctant to identify yourself as a Christian? In what sort of situation has this happened?

3. Why is our covenant relationship with God the foundation for everything in our walk with Him?

4. For the Christian, what is the relationship between "becoming righteous" and "doing good works"? How do some Christians get this backwards?

CHAPTER NINE

Understanding Delays

I was five years old when I went on my first trip to Disneyland. The 454-miles trip would take nine hours by car from our home in Northern California. My dad wanted to prepare me for how long this would be.

"Erik, this is going to be a long trip," he told me. "This will take all day. It will be dark when we get there, so you won't need to ask 'Are we there yet?'"

I got the message, "Okay, Dad," I said.

We got underway, and after I had exhausted all the ways I could find to amuse and entertain myself, and after enduring this endless road trip and sitting for what seemed like forever, I couldn't wait any longer.

I had to get an update.

"Dad are we there yet?"

We had gone 3 miles from home.

God, What's Taking So Long?

We haven't even left our city.

We still had 451 miles to go.

As a child I was like Donkey in *Shrek 2* on the journey to the kingdom of Far Far Away. Every trip we took I annoyed my parents with my constant refrain, "Are we there yet? Are we there yet?"

Now that I am older and more mature, I don't annoy my parents with that question any longer. But I have at times found myself asking God the same questions—"Are we there yet?" and "How much longer will it be?"—as I'm waiting to reach desired destinations in my life. Patience hasn't been my greatest virtue. God in His comfort encourages me with signs along the road: "Expect Delays."

We all have desired destinations we are driving toward in our life, but we must be prepared for and equipped to handle unexpected delays.

SOME PEOPLE SPEND THEIR WHOLE LIVES IN THE LAND OF TOMORROW AND NEVER LIVE IN TODAY.

The challenge we face in our culture is that we get "destination" disease. We get so focused on where we want to go that we lose sight of where we have been. We get discouraged by where we aren't and we forget to celebrate where we are.

I love this anonymous poem:

First I was dying to finish high school and start college.

And then I was dying to finish college and start
working.

And then I was dying to marry and have children.

And then I was dying for my children to grow old
enough for school

So I could return to work.

And then I was dying to retire.

And now I am dying.

And suddenly I realized I forgot to live.

We don't have yesterday, and tomorrow isn't here, so let's make the most of where we are at now. Let's live life to the full with delays and all. Some people spend their whole lives in the land of tomorrow and never live in today.

But how do I do that when my life feels like it is stuck for miles in non-moving traffic?

How to Handle a Delay

When we're faced with a delay, we can remain encouraged by seeing the big picture. Successful people live in today while seeing the bigger picture of tomorrow. Successful people don't think in days, weeks, or years—they think in decades.

SUCCESSFUL PEOPLE DON'T THINK IN DAYS, WEEKS, OR YEARS—THEY THINK IN DECADES.

God, What's Taking So Long?

GREAT MINDS CAN SEE PAST SHORT-TERM UPS AND DOWNS TO SEE THE LONG-TERM POTENTIAL.

Billionaire Sam Walton said, "I never invest in a company for where it will be in 18 months but for where it will be in 10 years." Great minds can see past short-term ups and down to see the long-term potential.

We may feel that our start is slow but it is more how we finish than how we start. We all will encounter unexpected delays that leave us wondering if we're ever going to get there. But when we see the bigger picture God has for our lives it empowers us to enjoy the journey, to maximize the moment, to not give up and to look past the delays.

There is a remarkable story in the Bible of a young man named Joseph. He experienced some pretty significant delays in his life. I encourage you to read his story beginning in Genesis 37.

Joseph was the eleventh son of his father Jacob, and Joseph's brothers were jealous of him because their Father favored him. One day Joseph dreamed that his brothers would bow down and honor him. He made the mistake of telling his brothers about this dream, and they hated him all the more. (It's not always wise to tell everyone your dreams.)

One day Joseph was sent by his father to check on his brothers in the fields and when they saw him they conspired to get rid of him. They grabbed him and threw him in a pit, and when a caravan of slave traders passed by, they sold Joseph into slavery. He was taken to Egypt, where he was sold to one of Pharaoh's officers named Potiphar.

Delay #1

This seems like a pretty big delay to me. You have a dream of being a leader and ruler, but instead your own brothers sell you into slavery.

Joseph didn't feel sorry for himself. Instead, he put his faith in God. God was with Joseph and caused him to succeed at everything he put his hand to. Joseph became the head administrator of Potiphar's house.

Delay #2

After a time, Potiphar's wife tried to seduce Joseph, but he remained faithful and she falsely accused him of sexual impropriety and he was thrown in prison.

Just when things were starting to look up, Joseph was thrown into prison, which was even worse than his previous situation. But God gave him a vision. In spite of these delays, he knew that somehow God would bring His Word to pass.

God was with Joseph and he had favor with the jailer—and soon he was running the prison for the head jailer.

Several years later, two of Pharaoh's servants were thrown into prison and both of them had dreams that

Joseph was able to interpret for them. One servant was executed, as Joseph predicted, and the other was restored to service.

Delay #3

The restored servant promptly forgot Joseph and he remained in prison another two years.

Joseph was sold by his brothers, lied about by Potiphar's wife, and thrown into prison. Everything that could go wrong had gone wrong, but he didn't lose sight of his dream and of God.

One night Pharaoh had a dream that no one could interpret. The restored servant suddenly remembered Joseph, who was immediately summoned by Pharaoh, and he successfully interpreted the dream—and he was promoted to the second-highest position in the land. In one hour he went from prison to the palace.

Several years later there was a terrible famine in the land, and Joseph's brothers—who did not recognize him—arrived in Egypt to buy grain and go to the palace, where they bowed before him.

Eventually Joseph revealed himself to his brothers. At first they were afraid he might have them killed. But Joseph was kind, and said, *"But as for you, you meant evil against me; but God meant it for good, in order to bring it about as it is this day, to save many people alive"* (Gen 50:20 *NKJV*).

Joseph saw the bigger picture that no matter how someone had wronged him or gotten in his way, God was still in control of his life. God would use the negative that people brought against him and turn it around for his good.

We need to be like Joseph and remember in those times when we feel people are getting in the way of our dreams, that God is bigger. God can take anything negative and turn it for our good.

God's Timing is Perfect

"And we know that all things work together for good to those who love God, to those who are the called according to His purpose" (Romans 8:28 *NKJV*).

No person can stand between you and God's dream destination for your life.

Sometimes we are slowed down in the journey of life due to timing issues. It has been estimated that we will spend six months of our lives waiting at traffic lights.

> NO PERSON CAN STAND BETWEEN YOU AND GOD'S DREAM DESTINATION FOR YOUR LIFE.

Sometimes it feels like God has us waiting at red lights. It may be the time is not right. The Bible says, *"To everything there is a season, a time for every purpose under heaven"* (Ecclesiastes 3:1 *NKJV*).

God, What's Taking So Long?

Sometimes we aren't where we want to be because the time is not right. We must learn to trust God and believe that He knows the right time. *"He has made everything beautiful in its time"* (Ecclesiastes 3:11 *NKJV*).

You'll recall I thought I was ready to get married when I was eighteen, but since Christy was only 13 at the time, I realized that God has a good handle on the subject of timing. We may feel ready on our end, but God may still be working out some timing issues on the other end.

Joseph could have been set free from prison after he interpreted the servant's dream, but at that point the best he could have expected was to be an ex-slave.

Instead, God had him wait two more years, until it was just the right time, and then within one hour he was promoted to the palace and became the vice-president of the most powerful nation in the world.

From this position God used him to save thousands from starvation and to play an important part in Israel's journey toward the Promised Land.

But we have to keep in mind that Joseph had to wait. From the day he had the dream until the day his dream was fulfilled, more than 20 years had passed.

Sometimes our wait is longer because God is preparing something even bigger for us than we imagined.

"And a wise man's heart discerns both time and judgment, because for every matter there is a time and judgment, though the misery of man increases greatly" (Ecclesiastes 8:5-6 *NKJV*).

If you know God called you where you are now, don't move until God releases you. If God gave you your job, stay until He releases you.

Years ago I took a position as a youth pastor in Cincinnati. Three months into it I realized it wasn't what they advertised and I was unhappy. I asked God to move me. He said, "Not yet." I had things to learn I would later need for when I would become pastor of my own church.

I wrestled with God that next year for Him to release me.

Finally I said, "God, I am not happy here, but what matters more to me than my happiness is doing Your will. If this is Your will, then I know this is the best place I can be. So I choose to be happy."

The following week our staff was at a conference and in the middle of a session I heard God say in my heart, "I release you. It is time to go." God's timing is perfect.

I called a friend and told him that God had released me from that position and asked if he knew any places that needed a youth pastor. He said, "As a matter of fact, last week I had a talk with my pastor about hiring you!"

I learned that this pastor had expressed interest in me, but he felt it would be unethical to contact me and solicit me away from another pastor. He said they would have to wait until I approached them.

Had I left the church in Cincinnati immediately, I would have missed the biggest opportunity of my life. Everything God is doing at my current church I learned during that next season of ministry. Had I left early and not waited on God, I would have missed one of the biggest opportunities of my ministry.

On this journey of life we can expect delays. The good news is that God is bigger than any of them

ON THIS JOURNEY OF LIFE WE CAN EXPECT DELAYS.

and when we trust and surrender to His will, nothing can keep us from getting to our dream destinations.

"Therefore humble yourselves under the mighty hand of God, that He may exalt you in due time, casting all your care upon Him, for He cares for you" (1 Peter 5:6-7 *NKJV*).

The Word of God instructs us to yield our life. Sometimes we are delayed because we haven't yielded our way to God. We want to do it our way rather than let God direct our steps. This can cause serious delays.

When we are not humbling ourselves and not yielding to God, we are really saying, "God, I know better than you."

Humility is saying, "God, I don't know it all and I am going to admit that Your way is best and I trust you." It's safe to do that because we know that God will exalt us in due time. And we know we can cast all our care upon Him, because He cares for us.

Discussion Questions

1. Review the delays Joseph experienced. Could he have accomplished God's purpose for his life if he had bypassed any of these delays?

2. Consider some of the delays you have experienced or are experiencing now. Do you believe God will use those delays in your life to accomplish His purposes in you?

3. Why is "destination disease"—being so focused on where we want to go that we lose sight of where we've been—such a tragic malady?

4. As you think about your life right now, do you believe you are generally where God wants you to be—living in your city, attending your church, married to your spouse, working at your job? Do you need to make any changes to get fully in line with God's will? Are you content to trust God and remain where you are until God releases you?

CHAPTER TEN

Finding the Answer

In a well-known survey, *Psychology Today* once asked 52,000 Americans, "What does it take to make you happy?"

As you can imagine, the answers varied, but the interesting thing is that most of them had something in common:

"I would be happy if I only had a larger house."

"I would be happy if I only had more money."

"I would be happy if I only had some better clothes."

"I will be happy when I get out of school."

"I will be happy when I get a job."

"I will be happy when I get married."

"I will be happy when I have kids."

"I will be happy when the kids leave home."

Did you notice that the most popular answers all seemed to deal with external issues? They all seem to be saying, "My happiness depends upon having the right circumstances. And, of course, the problem of attaching our happiness to our physical situation is that things are always changing.

I heard about a little girl who was with her grandfather as he read her a story. From time to time, she would take her eyes off the book and reach up to touch his wrinkled cheek. She was alternately stroking her own cheek, then his again. Finally, she spoke up. "Grandpa, did God make you?"

"Yes, Sweetheart," he answered. "God made me a long time ago."

"Oh," she paused. "Grandpa, did God make me too?"

"Yes, indeed, honey," he said. "God made you just a little while ago."

She thought about that a moment.

She said, "He's getting better at it, isn't He?"

THERE IS ALWAYS SOMEONE ELSE WHO IS SMARTER, RICHER, MORE TALENTED, AND BETTER LOOKING THAN YOU.

There is always someone else who is smarter, richer, more talented, and better looking than you. If happiness comes through our physical surroundings then we will never reach it because everything around us is changing.

Solomon, who had everything imaginable, once said, *"Whatever my eyes desired I did not keep from them. I did not withhold my heart from any pleasure...And indeed all was vanity and grasping for the wind"* (Ecclesiastes 2:10-11 *NKJV*).

He had everything, but it still wasn't enough to make him happy!

The first sermon Jesus taught was on happiness. Of all the subjects Jesus could have started with, He chose "How to Be Happy." Why?

HE HAD EVERYTHING, BUT IT STILL WASN'T ENOUGH TO MAKE HIM HAPPY!

Because He knew that everybody is searching for happiness.

His sermon began with the Beatitudes (from a Latin word meaning "blessed" or "happy").

> *"Blessed are the poor in spirit,*
> *For theirs is the kingdom of heaven.*
> *Blessed are those who mourn,*
> *For they shall be comforted.*
> *Blessed are the meek,*
> *For they shall inherit the earth.*
> *Blessed are those who hunger and thirst for righteousness,*
> *For they shall be filled."*
>
> —Matthew 5:3-6 *NKJV*

Notice that these are all inward qualities for happiness. Happiness, He said, results from a humble spirit, a tender heart, a craving for righteousness, and a merciful spirit. None of those qualities require the circumstances of our

OUR HAPPINESS IS NOT DETERMINED BY WHAT'S HAPPENING AROUND US, BUT RATHER BY WHAT'S HAPPENING IN US.

lives to be great. So even when circumstances are bad you can still be happy. Why? Because happiness is an inside job.

We often try to take a path that leads to happiness from the outside in, but God's path to happiness is from the inside out. Our happiness is not determined by what's happening around us, but rather by what's happening in us.

We can see this in the first Beatitude.

"Happy are the poor in spirit,
For theirs is the kingdom of heaven."

—Matthew 5:3 *NKJV*

What did Jesus mean by "poor in spirit"? It's not poor in the pocket book. He's not talking about low self-esteem or about putting yourself down. Jesus did not die for worthless junk—the cross shows your value to God.

Jesus was talking about humility. Humility means simply being totally dependent on God. I am truly humble when I admit that I don't have it all together, that I haven't arrived, that I haven't learned it all, and that I'm not God.

Over and over the Bible tells us it's possible to be happy regardless of what's going on around us—we can be happy because of what's going on within us. Happiness is found when we are dependent upon God, not independent from Him.

When we put our spiritual lives before our physical lives, we can be truly happy regardless of our circumstances.

That's why Paul and Silas, though they had been beaten and were in prison, could still praise God at the midnight hour (Acts 16).

That's why James could say, "Count it all joy when you encounter various trials" (James 1:2).

That's why Paul could write: *"And He said to me, 'My grace is sufficient for you, for My strength is made perfect in weakness.' Therefore most gladly I will rather boast in my infirmities, that the power of Christ may rest upon me...For when I am weak, then I am strong"* (2 Corinthians 12:9-10 *NKJV*).

True happiness, Jesus tells us, is from the inside out, not the outside in.

> TRUE HAPPINESS, JESUS TELLS US, IS FROM THE INSIDE OUT, NOT THE OUTSIDE IN.

Depending on God

Ordinarily, I am happier when I am full, not when I'm hungry. But when we are hungry for God, we are happy.

"Happy are those who hunger and thirst for righteousness,
For they shall be filled."

—Matthew 5:6 *NKJV*

God, What's Taking So Long?

Have you found yourself in a desert this past year, where you felt hungry and thirsty for something more? Does your life ever seem to get dry? God allows desert situations in our lives because He is trying to get our attention and let us know that our priorities are not right.

"So He humbled you, allowed you to hunger, and fed you with manna which you did not know nor did your fathers know, that He might make you know that man shall not live by bread alone; but man lives by every word that proceeds from the mouth of the Lord" (Deuteronomy 8:3 *NKJV*).

There are no Taco Bells in the Sinai wilderness. They got hungry and God provided manna. Notice that "God let them get hungry." He let them get hungry so they would recognize their need for Him and would depend on Him. God allows some things in our lives to get our attention. He is saying, "Look! What you want is not pleasure, not possessions, not performance. What you really want is Me. I made you with a God-shaped vacuum and I want to meet that need."

IF YOU'RE HUNGRY, THAT MEANS GOD IS GETTING READY TO DO SOMETHING IN YOUR LIFE!

"Then the Devil came and said to him, 'If you are the Son of God, change these stones into loaves of bread.' But Jesus told him, "No! The Scriptures say, 'People need more than bread for their life they must feed on every word of God'" (Matthew 4:3-4 *NLT*).

Happy are the hungry! If you're hungry, that means God is getting ready to do something in your life!

Finding the Answer

"And Jesus said to them, "I am the bread of life. He who comes to Me shall never hunger" (John 6:35 *NKJV*).

Bread is the basic essential of life. In a famine the first thing they unload is flour to make bread.

"Jesus answered and said to her, "Whoever drinks of this water will thirst again, but whoever drinks of the water that I shall give him will never thirst. But the water that I shall give him will become in him a fountain of water springing up into everlasting life" (John 4:13-14 *NKJV*).

Water is even more essential than food. You can go several weeks without food, but you can't go more than about three days without water. You cannot survive without water. Jesus is saying, "I'm like water—you need Me! You need Me to survive. I am the Living Water. I made you and you can't make it without Me!"

In Greek there are two words for "hungry." One means, "I'm hungry for a bite of something, I want a piece of bread." The other means, "I'm hungry for the whole loaf." Guess which word Jesus used here.

Jesus says "Happiness comes for people who say, 'I want all of God there is! I want to know Him in His fullness. I'm not satisfied with having a little blessing here or there. I want Him as the center of my life.'" That is the person who will be fully satisfied.

Many people aren't happy because they aren't hungry for God. They have filled up on spiritual junk food. Quit looking to things in life that don't satisfy and don't meet the need. What we are looking for is God! Let's quit wasting our time and our money on things of the world that really don't satisfy. Stop eating junk food!

You may need to go on a "media fast" to get your spiritual hunger back. When was the last time you were in your car with the radio turned off, just so you could talk to God while you're driving on the freeway? When was the last time you walked into your house and didn't automatically turn on the television?

The fact is that right now you are as close to God as you want to be. You can't blame it on anybody else. If you're not close to God right now, it's not God's fault, or your parent's fault, or your wife's fault, or your husband's fault, or your children's fault. You are as close to God as you want to be, because God always works in our lives according to our desires.

"Thus says the Lord: 'Cursed is the man who trusts in man and makes flesh his strength, whose heart departs from the Lord. For he shall be like a shrub in the desert, and shall not see when good comes, but shall inhabit the parched places in the wilderness in a salt land which is not inhabited'" (Jeremiah 17:5-6 *NJKV*).

The word used here for "shrub" in Hebrew is *arar* and refers to a specific tree in Israel that bears fruit. From a distance this tree and its fruit look beautiful. But if a hungry or thirsty traveler picks its attractive fruit, he will find a nasty surprise. When the fruit is opened, it is hollow and filled with webs and a dry pit. The tree is nicknamed the "cursed lemon" or the "Sodom apple" (it grows in the valley where God destroyed Sodom and Gomorrah). This plant is actually a type of milkweed that grows large hollow seedpods—the fruit looks good but really is empty inside.

God is saying that some people look good in their own flesh and power, but, apart from God, their success is dry and empty.

So don't stress if you are not sure about God's will. Your responsibility is to ask and seek, and it is God's responsibility to answer and show.

The Final Answer

What if you never get an answer to your prayer?

There is an interesting Jewish insight found in the very first verse of the book of Genesis. The first word in Genesis begins with the second letter of the Hebrew alphabet, *Bet.* The rabbis asked the question, "Why do the scriptures begin with the second letter of the alphabet rather than the first letter?" They concluded that this shows God doesn't have to answer every question and that not all knowledge is accessible to man, but some is reserved for God himself.

They pointed out that the shape of the letter *Bet* is "closed" on the right side but "open" on the left. Since Hebrew is read from the right to left, it appears that the scriptures start with a letter that is "open" to the direction of the reading, but closed to beginning of the text. Visually,

> YOU MAY NOT SEE THE ANSWER JUST YET, BUT KNOW THAT GOD HAS NOT LEFT YOU ALONE.

it's like a one-way sign indicating that you cannot go back, but you must start here and move forward.

You may not see the answer just yet, but know that God has not left you alone.

There is a legend of a Cherokee Indian youth's rite of passage. His father took him into the forest, blindfolded him and left him alone. He was required to sit silently on a stump the whole night and not remove the blindfold until morning. He could not cry out for help. If this boy survived the night, in the eyes of his tribe he had become a man. He could not tell the other boys of this experience, because each lad must come into manhood on his own.

The boy was naturally terrified. He heard many noises. Wild beasts must surely have been surrounding him, and maybe even some humans that might do him harm. There was a storm in the distance and the wind blew the grass and leaves around him. But this boy sat stoically, never removing the blindfold. He knew this was the only way he could become a man.

Finally, the horrific night ended and when the boy felt the sun shining on his face, he removed his blindfold.

It was then that he discovered his father sitting on the stump next to him. He had been at watch the entire night, protecting his son from harm.

Finding the Answer

We, too, are never alone.

Even when we don't know it, God is watching over us, sitting on the stump beside us. When trouble comes, all we have to do is reach out to Him.

Discussion Questions

1. How is humility—being "poor in spirit"—different from being financially poor or suffering from low self-esteem? What would be different about your life if you aspired to be humble?

2. Are there any "external" things you can name that you think might make you significantly more happy than you are right now? Are the things included in the promises of God—can you pray and ask God for them? If you never have them, will you always be unhappy?

3. Is it possible that you have a spiritual hunger that is being satiated by something other than God—relationships, media, addictions, etc.? Do you think a brief fast from that thing might be helpful for your spiritual development?

4. Are you feeling a spiritual hunger in your life right now? Do you think God may be about to do something big in your life? What do you think it might be?

PART TWO

Wait for the LORD
and keep his way.
He will exalt you...
—Psalm 37:34 *NIV*

First we pray, then what? What should we be doing while we are waiting on God to answer our prayers? Here are some practical suggestions for three common prayer requests.

CHAPTER ELEVEN

Waiting for Your Marriage

You may be praying about a problem in your marriage and wondering, "God, why is it taking so long for my spouse to get it together?"

By now you've realized that you cannot change your spouse—God will have to work that miracle—but while you are waiting on God, you can begin by changing yourself.

When we pray about our marriages, it's just like praying about anything else—we have to do our part. We need to do what we can do and let God do what He can do. And as you make some changes on the things you can control, you just might find you're starting to see some changes in the areas you can't control!

First of all, we need to keep in mind there are no perfect marriages because there are no perfect people.

Ralph seemed to have the perfect marriage, so on the Sunday before his 50th wedding anniversary his pastor

WE NEED TO KEEP IN MIND THERE ARE NO PERFECT MARRIAGES BECAUSE THERE ARE NO PERFECT PEOPLE.

decided to use him as a sermon illustration. Just before the pastor began his message, he asked Ralph to join him in front of the congregation.

"Please share some of your insight with us, Ralph," the pastor said. "How have you managed to live successfully with the same woman all those years?"

Ralph nodded thoughtfully as he took the microphone. "I always treated my wife with respect," he said. "And I always tried to show her she was valuable by spending money on her." He paused for a moment. "But I'd say the biggest secret to our happiness over the past fifty years was that I took her traveling."

"Traveling!" the pastor said. "Where did you go on these trips?"

"For our 25th anniversary," Ralph said, "I took her to Beijing, China."

The congregation applauded.

"Wow!" the pastor said. "What a great example you are for all of us husbands! So, tell us, Ralph, where will you be going for your 50th anniversary?"

Ralph said, "I'm going to go back to China to get her."

Three Keys to a Great Marriage

1. Put God First

The most important key to a successful relationship is your personal walk with God. True intimacy is not merely about becoming one physically, it's about becoming one spiritually— *"what God has joined together..."* (Matthew 19:6).

Our relationship must begin with God at the center. When God created Adam and Eve, it was Adam, Eve and God. He walked with them in the cool of the day. He was a daily part of their life together. God never intended for their relationship to work without Him.

As you'll recall, it was Adam and God before it was Adam and Eve. God—not our spouse—is our true source of fulfillment.

When someone becomes overly needy they become unattractive. Research has found that one of the primary traits of attractiveness is confidence. We admire people who are self-assured and focused—not cocky or arrogant, but confident. As believers, our confidence comes from God.

> GOD—NOT OUR SPOUSE—IS OUR TRUE SOURCE OF FULFILLMENT.

Perhaps you're familiar with the account of the woman at the well (see John 4:4-42). This woman had gone through five husbands and was now living with someone who was not her husband.

God, What's Taking So Long?

DO YOU THINK IT'S FAIR TO SAY THAT MOST PEOPLE LOVE US BASED ON WHAT THEY DON'T KNOW?

On this particular day she was alone at the well. No one wanted to be with her because her past was so bad. Do you think it's fair to say that most people love us based on what they don't know? If everyone knew everything about us, it would drastically shrink our list of friends. But when all your friends walk away, Jesus walks up.

Jesus said to the woman, "Please give me a drink."

She was shocked that He would even talk with her.

He said, "If you knew who you were talking to, you would ask for living water."

Jesus was saying, "You are looking for fulfillment in a man. If you would change wells, I would meet that need in a way no one else could ever meet it!"

The first thing you can do to improve your marriage is to put God first.

Put God first in your day by beginning every morning with devotions.

Put God first in your week by going to church.

Put God first in your finances—you can see where your heart is by looking in your checkbook.

Put God first in your problems—the sexiest thing you can do with your spouse is to pray together.

2. Become Soul Mates Second

Contrary to what you've seen in the movies and on TV, soul mates are made, not born. The greatest marriages are forged in the trenches, as two people slug it out together and over time their friendship deepens. A great marriage is about a covenant and not a contract. Eve was cut from Adam's side as a sign of cutting the covenant.

You've heard this before, but *marriage takes work.*

> YOU'VE HEARD THIS BEFORE, BUT MARRIAGE TAKES WORK.

Competing in the Olympics takes work. Earning a college degree takes work. Getting a promotion takes work. So why would we think building a good marriage should be easy and not take much work?

"Therefore shall a man leave his father and his mother, and shall cleave unto his wife: and they shall be one flesh" (Genesis 2:24 *KJV*).

The word "cleave" in our language may make us think of a meat cleaver, but in Hebrew it has the connotation of working at something. It means to "continually pursue."

As men, our nature is to pursue something—to conquer it, bag it, tag it, mount it and move on. But to "cleave" to our wives, we men must "continually pursue" them. What we did to get our woman we keep doing to keep her! Ladies, what you did to get your man you must continue to do to keep him!

LADIES, WHAT YOU DID TO GET YOUR MAN YOU MUST CONTINUE TO DO TO KEEP HIM!

Maybe you're thinking, "I just don't feel in love anymore. I've lost that loving feeling."

So what? Get it back! Keep it!

"Nevertheless I have this against you, that you have left your first love. Remember therefore from where you have fallen; repent and do the first works..." (Revelation 2:4-5 *NKJV*).

On airplanes they say in the event of an emergency you should place an oxygen mask on yourself and then try to help your child and those around you. If your marriage is losing altitude, first put the mask on yourself.

Begin by doing what you need to do. This is the **Law of Priority.** *"For this cause shall a man leave his father and mother."* You have to let go of some things. What are you leaving behind to pursue your spouse? You can have a career and hobbies and friends, but they can't be the most important part of your life—you must give your spouse first place. If you're a man, your mother comes after your wife. If you're a woman, your kids come after your husband.

If you're a man, it's your job to pursue your wife. As a husband, one of the most important things you can do for your wife is foreplay—but you need to remember that fore-play is spelled "R-O-M-A-N-C-E."

Romance is foreplay for a woman. To be successful at foreplay you need to stop being predictable. If she knows what you want the moment you touch her, you need to change your approach.

Turn foreplay into a 24-hour deal. Start "slow-roasting" your woman.

Do something nice for her. Then walk away.

Kiss her. Then walk away.

Give her a back rub. Then walk away.

Every woman is different when it comes to what she would consider romantic. So it's your job to study your wife and learn what she likes, wants and needs. In the same way that hunters study deer and fishermen study fish, study your woman. Just keep in mind that you want to track her, not stalk her.

Clear Communication

One of the most important keys to becoming soul mates with your spouse is clear communication. In fact, I'd say that the number one problem I've seen over and over as I've counseled married couples is poor communication.

"A brother offended is harder to win than a strong city, and contentions are like the bars of a castle" (Proverbs 18:19 *NKJV*).

A new wife baked cinnamon rolls for the first time, using a favorite family recipe handed down to her from her grandmother. As soon as they came out of the oven, she called her husband into the kitchen and served him a warm cinnamon roll and a glass of cold milk. She sat across from him at the table and watched excitedly as he took his first bite.

"If I baked these cinnamon rolls commercially," she asked, "how much do you think I could get for them?"

The husband swallowed and then took a sip of milk.

"10-12 years," he said.

"Husbands, love your wives, just as Christ also loved the church and gave Himself for her, that He might sanctify and cleanse her with the washing of water by the word, that He might present her to Himself a glorious church, not having spot or wrinkle or any such thing, but that she should be holy and without blemish" (Ephesians 5:25-27 *NKJV*).

We see here that Jesus uses his words to remove the blemishes and the wrinkles from our life. When we use our words in healthy ways, our communication cleanses and washes our perspective.

Notice that this verse is addressed to men and not women. Why? Perhaps it's because women don't have to be told to communicate. It comes naturally for them. It's the men who have to be told to communicate.

I'd bet there are not many husbands who regularly take their wives aside and say, "Would you just talk to me?"

Over the years I've observed that women feel a much stronger need to communicate than men do—and it frustrates them that communication is their need but not their husband's need. Ask a woman to describe her ideal man and she will describe another woman.

But before anyone accuses me of beating up on men for not being women, I want to point out that men and women are wired differently.

There are at least three reasons why women need to communicate.

First, women tend to process problems out loud while men tend to process internally. Men often want to be alone to think through an issue, but women will work on finding a solution by talking about it. The longer she talks, the more likely she is to find the solution.

Secondly, communication is a woman's way to say she is crazy about her man. Many men make a huge mistake by thinking, "I wish I could just get some peace and quiet around here." If you notice that your wife used to talk to you all the time and now she isn't quite as talkative, that isn't a good thing. When she stops talking, you should be hearing an alarm!

Finally, communication is the deepest, most powerful way a wife experiences intimacy with her husband. This is a *need*—not just a *want*—of your wife. Husband, your wife's emotional need for *talk* is as strong as your need for *sex*. You may never fully understand why, but she needs to be able to share what is going on in her life. The road to intimacy for your wife is often long and winding. She wants to take the scenic route, not the interstate. Men want to get to the point—"I just want the bottom line," they say. "Is there a problem you need me to fix?"

God, What's Taking So Long?

One of the reasons we don't communicate more may be because we are so different in how we communicate. It's like we speak two different languages.

The best book I have seen on this subject is *Love & Respect* by Dr. Emerson Eggerichs. He says that men and women speak "in code." When a woman says, "I have nothing to wear," that's code for "I have nothing new." But when a man says, "I have nothing to wear," that's code for "I have nothing clean."

"Judge not, that you be not judged. For with what judgment you judge, you will be judged; and with the measure you use, it will be measured back to you. And why do you look at the speck in your brother's eye, but do not consider the plank in your own eye? Or how can you say to your brother, 'Let me remove the speck from your eye'; and look, a plank is in your own eye? Hypocrite! First remove the plank from your own eye, and then you will see clearly to remove the speck from your brother's eye" (Matthew 7:1-5 *NJKV*).

SO OFTEN WE JUDGE OTHER PEOPLE BY THEIR ACTIONS, WHILE AT THE SAME TIME WE WANT THEM TO JUDGE US BY OUR INTENTIONS.

Communication problems in marriages are not limited to husbands who do not communicate or do not communicate tactfully. There are wives who do not communicate properly or who communicate destructively. The starting place for healthy communication is to stop trying to get them to understand you before you start trying to understand them.

We need to stop judging others. When we appear to have a conflict, it may be helpful to assume that what we have is a misunderstanding. So often we judge other people by their *actions,* while at the same time we want them to judge us by our *intentions.*

Although you can always improve your ability to communicate with your spouse, let's take a look at seven secrets that will help you kick-start successful communication.

1. *Commit to Communicate*

"*...Speaking the truth in love, may grow up in all things...* " (Ephesians 4:15 *NKJV*).

Ladies, contrary to popular belief, men cannot read your minds. When we do something wrong and we get that blank look on our faces, we really don't know what we did.

"You know what you did."

"I don't know."

"Don't play dumb with me"

"Give me a hint."

"If you don't know then I'm not telling you."

Please, ladies—help us help you!

2. *Set a Time for Communication*

"Do not let any unwholesome talk come out of your mouths, but only what is helpful for building others up according to their needs, that it may benefit those who listen" (Ephesians 4:29 *NIV*).

In communication, timing is critical. Ladies, perhaps you've noticed when your husband comes home from work that he is not very talkative. But you haven't seen him all day and you're ready to start talking the moment he walks through the door.

You say, "How was your day?"

He says, "Fine."

"Anything interesting happen today?"

"Nothing new."

Your husband may need time to unwind after work before he can have meaningful conversation with you. Remember, deep conversation is your need—not his. You should also keep in mind that it's been said that women use 50,000 words a day and men use 20,000—it could be that your husband has used up most of his words at work.

Sir, perhaps you've been trying to make time to communicate more with your wife, but she still seems dissatisfied with your effort. Let me give you a few practical tips that will help you become a better communicator:

- Don't multitask or try to squeeze in your talking during commercials.

- Keep appropriate eye contact and nod every once in awhile (not the autopilot nod).

- Repeat key thoughts to show you have heard her.

- Keep your body language open. Don't cross your arms or keep looking at your watch.

- Validate her feelings by asking "feeling" questions: "How did that make you feel?" "Was that hard for you?" "Didn't that make you angry?"

3. Choose Words That Build Rather than Divide

"Do not let any unwholesome talk come out of your mouths..." (Ephesians 4:29 *NIV*).

Don't use abusive language. Avoid sentences like "You have two brains—one is lost and the other is out looking for it!"

Don't use extreme language. Avoid saying things like "You never..." or "You always..." If you believe your wife will never change, she may start to feel the same way and she will give up!

4. Invite God into the Conversation

"And do not grieve the Holy Spirit of God, with whom you were sealed for the day of redemption" (Ephesians 4:30 *NIV*).

As soon as you realize a problem is escalating—STOP! Take a moment to say, "Let's invite God into this to help us resolve this." Remember that God is present and He has been listening to your conversation. Take a Bible break!

5. Don't Attack

"Get rid of all bitterness, rage and anger, brawling and slander, along with every form of malice" (Ephesians 4:31 *NIV*).

If you and your spouse have an honest disagreement about a legitimate issue, focus on the issue—not the other person!

6. Forgive and Forget

"Be kind and compassionate to one another, forgiving each other, just as in Christ God forgave you" (Ephesians 4:32 *NIV*).

Our heavenly Father has forgiven us of so much and He treats us with love and mercy—as though we had never sinned against Him. That's how we should treat others.

7. Encourage Progress, No Matter How Small

"Do not despise these small beginnings, for the Lord rejoices to see the work begin" (Zechariah 4:10 *NLT*).

When we try to change we will most likely not get it right the first fifty times. But encourage one another on every attempt. "That was almost a good thing you did." Affirm your spouse's efforts even when they fall short. Say, "Thank you" or "Good try." Don't say, "It's about time" or "Is that the best you can do?"

3. Become Bed-Mates Third

How often has a wife said something like this to her husband: "Not tonight, Honey. I am just too tired!"?

Here's what she really said to her husband: "You get the leftovers of my energy. The kids are more important than you. My job is more important. The housework is more important. The errands are more important."

Of course all those things have value—and after a busy day of handling all those things, she probably is too tired—but basically she's telling him she had time and energy for everything else. She is communicating that he is not number one in her life. Generally speaking, we find time for what we consider important. It's the *Law of Priority*.

Many wives are aware of their man's strong sex drive, but they don't respect it. Don't make your husband feel dirty because he wants sex more than you do. God created

DON'T MAKE YOUR HUSBAND FEEL DIRTY BECAUSE HE WANTS SEX MORE THAN YOU DO.

God, What's Taking So Long?

him with a strong sex drive. Just as romance is glue for you, sex is glue for him—and it keeps him pursuing you.

As a wife, you need to understand that you are God's only legitimate way for your husband's sexual needs to be met. So when you dismiss your husband's interest in sex with you and refuse to meet his sexual needs, you are opening the door to temptation for him.

Of course he is ultimately responsible for his actions, and nothing justifies sexual immorality. But you hold the key—and by meeting your husband's sexual needs, you help lock the door on temptation.

Finally, as you continue to pray about your marriage, I encourage you to expect a miracle. Approach your situation optimistically. Keep reminding yourself that you are being faithful in doing your part and that God is being faithful in doing His part. Praying for your marriage is just like praying about anything else—we do what only we can do and we let God do what only He can do!

Discussion Questions

1. Do you think it's fair to say that most people love others based on what they don't know about them? If everyone knew everything about you, would you be concerned that this would drastically shrink your list of friends? Since God knows everything about you, how does that affect your relationship with Him?

2. Can you identify some of the things you did initially to "get" your spouse? Do some of those things now feel like a chore to do to "keep" your spouse?

3. Can you think of a situation where your spouse has been critical of your "action" but has overlooked your "intention"? Was this a matter of poor communication—did your spouse not understand or properly interpret your action? Or was it more a matter of you failing to follow through on your good intention?

4. Why is it important for you to approach your marriage situation with expectancy and optimism? Why is it important for your spouse that you do? Why is it important to God that you have this attitude?

CHAPTER TWELVE

Waiting for Your Finances

You may be praying about a money problem wondering, "God, why is it taking You so long to meet my financial needs?"

Let me begin by encouraging you that you are not alone if you are facing financial challenges. Experts say that 45% of American workers have money trouble (that's nearly half of us) and 15% have serious money problems. In over twenty years of ministry, I've been asked about money matters more than any other issue.

So what should you be doing while you are waiting on God to honor His promise to bless you financially?

Let's look at some principles in God's Word that you may have overlooked or neglected.

First, I want to remind you that God cares and He wants to help you. He is not a stingy Father as some people wrongly think.

Johnny was in math class and his teacher asked him to solve a problem on the chalkboard.

"Johnny, if you had five dollars and you asked your father for three dollars more, how many dollars would you have?"

"I would have five dollars," Johnny said.

"You don't know your arithmetic," the teacher said.

"You don't know my father," Johnny said.

You may have an earthly father like Johnny's, but your heavenly Father isn't stingy with His children.

"Let them shout for joy and be glad...and let them say continually, 'Let the Lord be magnified, who has pleasure in the prosperity of His servant'" (Psalms 35:27 *NKJV*).

Perhaps you're wondering why we would look to the Bible for answers to our money problems. Isn't the Bible just about spiritual stuff like prayer and faith?

Many people are surprised to learn that the Bible has a lot to say about money—in fact, the Bible talks about money and money management more than any other subject. For example, the Bible contains approximately 500 verses on prayer and less than 500 verses on faith, but more than 2,300 verses on money and possessions—that's four times more!

Let's begin by examining a foundational financial principle that the Bible calls "stewardship." This is not a word used much in our language today. A word we use that would mean the same thing is "management." According to the Bible, everyone is in management. We are either managing our money or we are managing a crisis.

You may be thinking, "I don't need a lesson in managing money—I just need a lot more money to manage!" Maybe you've heard about how to calculate the cost of living—just take your income and add 15%.

But what would you think of a person who was struggling with basic addition problems, yet says to the teacher, "Let's get right into algebra!"? Or what about the person who can't swim but is getting bored standing around in the shallow water and says, "Let's go into the deep water!"?

We would think their elevator is stuck in the basement. But how often do we do that same thing with money—"I can't manage what I have, but go ahead and give me more because I'm sure I could do it then!"

STATISTICS SHOW THAT SOMETHING LIKE 80% OF ALL LOTTERY WINNERS FILE BANKRUPTCY WITHIN FIVE YEARS.

If more money was the answer, why do so many lottery winners go from broke to rich back to broke? Statistics show that something like 80% of all lottery winners file bankruptcy within five years.

More money isn't the answer—the answer is better money management skills. Why should God give you more of His money if you can't manage what He has already given you?

IN FACT, WE NEED TO RECOGNIZE THAT GOD WON'T GIVE US MORE MONEY THAN WE CAN MANAGE.

In fact, we need to recognize that God won't give us more money than we can manage. He looks at our current ability and gives us what we can handle. What about people who have more than they can handle—like someone who wins the lottery or gains a large inheritance? Before long their wealth adjusts to the level they can lift.

"For the kingdom of heaven is like a man traveling to a far country, who called his own servants and delivered his goods to them. And to one he gave five talents, to another two, and to another one, to each according to his own ability; and immediately he went on a journey" (Matthew 25:14-15 *NKJV*).

In this parable we see that the Lord entrusted His possessions to His managers. He owned it and His servants managed it. He supplied the resources—without Him, the servants had nothing. If the servants thought they were the owners of the goods, they needed to do some serious reevaluation.

That's how it is for us, too.

"For the earth is the Lord's, and all its fullness" (1 Corinthians 10:26 *NKJV*). Everything in this earth belongs to God. *"'The silver is Mine, and the gold is Mine,' says the Lord of hosts"* (Haggai 2:80 *NKJV*). We aren't owners; we are just managers.

God is looking at how we handle worldly wealth to see if we are trustworthy of greater riches in His kingdom.

"So take the talent from him, and give it to him who has ten talents. For to everyone who has, more will be given, and he will have abundance; but from him who does not have, even what he has will be taken away" (Matthew 25:28-29 *NKJV*).

Some people seem to think their main task in life is to get rid of money as fast as they get it. It's like they're playing hot potato whenever they get a paycheck. But God is looking for fruitfulness. He told Adam and Eve, "Be fruitful and multiply." Jesus rebuked the fig tree that didn't bear fruit. One day you and I will stand before the Lord and have an audit of how we managed His money. And God will reward increase.

> ONE DAY YOU AND I WILL STAND BEFORE THE LORD AND HAVE AN AUDIT OF HOW WE MANAGED HIS MONEY.

Simple Steps toward Better Money Management

The whole prospect of managing money can be intimidating, but if our life goals include financial increase, we need to learn how to manage what we have.

"The plans of the diligent lead to profit as surely as haste leads to poverty" (Proverbs 21:5 *NIV*).

Do you have a definite plan mapped out for your financial future? It seems like some of us put more planning into our vacations than we do our financial freedom or retirement. It's like we've planned the wedding but haven't given any thought to the marriage. We wouldn't dream of building a house without a plan, but we don't think twice about making spending decisions that could potentially impact our family's overall financial strategy.

FIRST YOU NEED TO KNOW WHERE YOU ARE, AND THEN YOU WILL KNOW WHAT YOU NEED TO CHANGE TO GET YOU WHERE YOU WANT TO GO.

Begin by balancing the books. Take stock of what you've got. First you need to know where you are, and then you will know what you need to change to get you where you want to go.

"Be sure you know the condition of your flocks, give careful attention to your herds; for riches do not endure forever, and a crown is not secure for all generations" (Proverbs 27:23-24 *NIV*).

One of the important principles to keep in mind when you're getting started is that you can't manage what you can't measure. In business we set benchmarks and establish *KPIs ("Key Performance Indicators")* to help measure progress and keep us on track. If this is good for running a profitable business, shouldn't we do the same thing with something as important as our financial life?

So your first step is to gather some information. *"Get the facts at any price"* (Proverbs 23:23 *LB*).

Waiting for Your Finances

1. **Make a list of what you own.** You don't have to include your toothbrush on this list, but do take stock of all your major possessions—home, cars, bank accounts, furniture, professional wardrobe, investments, etc.

2. **Make a list of what you earn.** Calculate your annual total and break it down to what you earn every month.

3. **Make a list of what you owe.** Calculate what it would take to pay off everything you owe—your school loans, your cars, your credit cards, etc. If you could take care of everything by writing one check, how big would that check be?

   (If you have a mortgage, you may not wish to include that amount in your calculations. A mortgage is a special kind of debt because, ordinarily, at any time your house will be worth more than what you owe on it—so the moment you sell your property, that debt is eliminated.)

   Then make a list of your current monthly expenses. Include your regular bills (telephone, power, etc.) and any debt repayment (automobile payments, minimum credit card payments, etc.). If you have any bills you pay every other month or several times a year (automobile insurance, renter insurance, etc.), you may find it helpful to calculate the annual total owed and break that down into monthly amounts.

4. **Make a list of where it goes.** A quick comparison between your "earn" list with your "owe" list will tell

ARE YOU KEEPING YOUR HEAD ABOVE WATER—OR ARE YOU SINKING FAST?

you part of the story right now. Are you keeping your head above water—or are you sinking fast?

If things look good for you, I want to encourage you to keep reading this chapter—we can all make improvements on our money management. On the other hand, if the numbers aren't exactly where you want them to be, I want to remind you that we still haven't factored in the promises of God.

"And my God shall supply all your need according to His riches in glory by Christ Jesus" (Philippians 4:19 *NKJV*).

What you need to do next will take some discipline, but it's important. Keep a record of what you're actually spending your money on for one month. Write it down every day. Make accurate notes of all of your expenditures—every check in the mail, every credit card swipe, every tank of gas, every cup of coffee, every trip to the grocery store, every vending machine purchase.

Your first response may be, "I don't have time for that much record-keeping." Who does? But if you spend 40 or more hours of your life each week making money, isn't it worth a few minutes a day tracking where it goes?

Once you start documenting how you actually spend your money, you may be amazed at how much money you waste. You may feel that money is tight, but then you discover you're eating out four nights a week or that you only watch a few programs on TV every week but you're paying for 1500 channels. Making a few minor changes can be an easy way to find a surprising amount of extra money.

The second step to good money management is to create a budget. That's right—*you need to create a budget.* Don't let that word bother you—a budget is nothing more than your personal spending plan. Some people approach creating a budget with the same enthusiasm they have for working on their taxes. (Have you heard the good news? The IRS has simplified our tax return forms for next year by reducing them to two sections. In the first section you write in how much money you made last year. In the second section you find out where to send it.)

Wise money management requires a realistic spending plan. If your outgo exceeds your income then your upkeep will be your downfall. There are a lot of ways to plan your spending and many great systems to help you develop a budget, so go to the library or go online and in a few minutes of searching you'll find plenty of great examples and tools.

In a nutshell, the key to developing an effective budget is looking at three categories.

God, What's Taking So Long?

- Needs
- Wants
- Desires

We *need* to eat. We *want* to eat at a restaurant. We *desire* to eat lobster.

Do you get the distinction?

We *need* a place to live. We *want* a house with three bedrooms. We *desire* a house with four bedrooms and a three-car garage.

Learning the difference between these three levels will help you set a realistic budget as you cut costs by trimming back on *desires* and *wants* and begin to focus on *needs*.

A budget helps you stay on track to reach your financial goals. Have you ever seen a kid in the store scream until Mommy gives him what he wants? There are adults just like that kid. A couple agrees on a reasonable budget and they keep it until one person sees something they just have to have and start throwing a tantrum until the other person gives in.

My observation is that women tend to nickel and dime a budget to death.

"I've got to get a new hairdo."

"Why?"

"To go with my new belt"

"Why?"

'To match the new shoes I got for 20% off."

Guys do this too, but generally men will kill the budget all at once.

"Baby, look at these new Ping golf clubs!"

"Hey, there's a sale on his and her Jet skis!"

You can't get out of a hole if you keep shoveling. Stop digging. Stop spending money you don't have. Pray before you pay. Say "NO" for a little while so you can say "YES" for the rest of your life.

The third step to good money management is to get out of debt. Depending on your situation, it may help to do some plastic surgery on yourself. Get out your credit cards and cut them up. Credit card company studies show you will spend 23% more if you use credit than if you use cash. Credit cards make it easier to buy things you can't afford and don't need.

"The wise have wealth and luxury, but fools spend whatever they get" (Proverbs 21:20 *NLT*).

Fools spend whatever they get—and a fool with a credit card spends money he doesn't even have. *Ouch!* Been there and done that.

Personally, I like to use a debit card. But if you need to keep a credit card for reserving air tickets and rental cars or whatever, perhaps you should keep it in a place where you can't easily access it and risk using it to buy unnecessary things. For example, you could freeze your credit card in a large bowl filled with water. Then when you need it, pull it out and let it thaw. This will give you time to make sure you are not making an impulse purchase. (However, if your first thought when you heard this suggestion was "microwave," perhaps it's not a good idea for you to keep a credit card!)

You may be wondering how to function without a credit card. I'm suggesting you do something strange. Use cash. I'm serious. It's still accepted most places.

If you decide to keep a credit card or two, you should take a look at how much in interest you are paying every month. The average American carries four credit cards with balances of $9,000-$13,000, often with interest rates of 18%-21%. You might be surprised at how much your "convenience" is costing you.

It's possible that in your present financial situation you already have the money you need, but you are just spending too much of it on the interest on your credit card and automobile payments. So before you start praying for God to give you more money, start being more faithful with what you have—by getting out of debt.

Let's look at an example of an average person with $8,100 in credit card debt.

Debt	Total Owed	Minimum Payment
Sears 18%	$600	$24
Dillard's 18%	$1,200	$48
Master Card 18%	$1,500	$60
Visa 18%	$1,800	$72
Discover 18%	$3,000	$120

This person is paying $324 a month in minimum payments. This will take 11.1 years to pay off and will cost $4,438 in interest. Remember, it's not only the interest that you pay but also the interest that you lose. If this person had invested those same monthly payments at 12%, in 11 years it would have grown to $88,000.

Also, you need to keep in mind that the car you drive is a million dollar decision. The average car payment is $378 dollars. Most people never pay off their cars but keep trading in for new ones. But if you took $378 at age 25 and invested it every month at 12%, when you reached age 65 you'd have almost 4.5 million dollars. If you've been spending $500 a month in car payments, over the next 40 years you could build a nest egg of $6 million dollars!

But even if it takes the average person 11.1 years or longer to pay off their credit cards, I'm going to show you how to pay down your debt much faster. Are you ready to be debt free?

First, see if you can find an extra $50 a month—buy less coffee or take a bag lunch to work one or two days each week. Second, sell something you can't afford. Maybe you bought a car for status reasons that you can't really afford. Cars aren't meant for status but transportation. If you're serious about getting out of debt, sell that car and get one that's less expensive.

Then you are going to add that extra $50 to your credit card payment with the lowest *balance*. As soon as the credit card with the lowest balance is paid off, you're going to begin adding that entire payment to the credit card with the next *lowest* balance.

Debt	Total Owed	Minimum Payment	New Payment
Sears 18%	$600	$24	$24 + $50 = $74
Dillard's 18%	$1,200	$48	$48 + $74 = $122
Master Card 18%	$1,500	$60	$60 + $122 = $182
Visa 18%	$1,800	$72	$72 + $182 = $254
Discover 18%	$3,000	$120	$120 + $254 = $374

YOU'LL BE AMAZED AT HOW FAST YOU CAN OVERCOME YOUR INDEBTEDNESS.

You'll be amazed at how fast you can overcome your indebtedness. Since you've started paying cash for your purchases and you're not accumulating any more debt, you'll be debt-free in 2.8 years (saving yourself 8 years!) and you'll have an extra $374 a month that you can painlessly invest for your future!

Go to the ant, you sluggard!
Consider her ways and be wise,

Waiting for Your Finances

Which, having no captain,

Overseer or ruler,

Provides her supplies in the summer,

and gathers her food in the harvest.

—Proverbs 6:6-8 *NKJV*

A guy asked his buddy, "How much money do you have in the bank?"

"I don't know," he said, "I haven't shaken it in a while."

An ant would tell you it's wise to bank your extra money. Sometimes people will come to me and say, "I really want to save, but I don't have any extra money."

"Well," I always ask them, "do you think you could find an extra five dollars? What about skipping that expensive coffee you have every day on the way to work? What about bringing a brown bag lunch instead of eating out every day?"

"But that's only five dollars," they say.

"Only five dollars?" I say. "Five dollars a day invested at a 12% return for five years is $12,000. Invest five dollars a day for ten years and you'll have $34,000, over twenty years you'll have $150,000, over thirty years you'll have $500,000, and over forty years you'll have over $1.7 million."

If you start investing five dollars a day when you are 25, and keep doing it until you are 75, you would have nearly six million dollars. Just think what you could do for God and your family with $6 million!

God, What's Taking So Long?

"The wise man saves for his future" (Proverbs 21:20a *LB*).

Set a goal to have at least $1,000 for emergencies. Keep this money in a savings account. Who knows, God may use this money to supply your needs according to His riches in glory at some future time. How small is your faith to think that God only supplies *after* the need? He may be supplying your need before you even knew you had a need.

Too many times, however, God saw the need coming and tried to cover you, but you went out and blew it because you have a zero-balance mentality.

Beginning today, whenever you want to make a purchase, save the money in advance. Begin saving for purchases and spending cash on them rather than charging them on a credit card. So if you picked out a nice Christmas gift for your wife at Bass Pro, start saving now so you can pay cash. The holidays are particularly dangerous financially. It takes the average consumer eight months to pay off the debt they accumulated between Thanksgiving and New Year's Eve.

"The wise have wealth and luxury, but fools spend whatever they get" (Proverbs 21:20 *NLT*).

Once you have eliminated your debt (with the exception of your house) and you have $1,000 set aside, your next goal should be to save three to six months of living expenses. Put this in something liquid, like a high-yielding money market account. You want your emergency living expenses in a liquid account in case you lose your job and need quick access to your money. If you have your money in stocks or mutual funds, and you've lost your job because the markets are in a down turn, you'd be pulling your investment out at a down time and miss out on profits and growth.

And finally, after you've got your "emergency fund" in a savings account and several months of living expenses in place, it's time to start paying off your home!

Money + Time + Consistency = Wealth.

Wealth isn't what you make, but what you manage to save from what you make. It is really simple. If you make $50,000 and spend $50,000, how much money do you have? If you make $500,000 this year and spend $500,000, are you really wealthy?

It may help to look at your dollars like they are employees. If you want, you can fire them—fire them at the mall, at the shoe store, or fire them by making interest payments. Or you can send them to work for you.

Whenever you invest your money, your money is working for you—working to make more money for you. When you spend fifty dollars, you didn't just lose that fifty dollars, you also lost the potential that fifty dollars had to earn for you (which over thirty years at 12% would be $1,800). If you needlessly fire a fifty-dollar employee every month, over the next thirty years you'd be losing the power to earn $176,000.

Building wealth is as simple as eating an apple. An apple provides for my immediate physical needs and it also provides for my future needs. Twenty percent of an apple is the core, but at the core are the seeds to create more apple trees. In the same way, every dollar has the seeds for your next harvest. Stop eating your future!

"Enjoy what you have rather than desiring what you don't have" (Ecclesiastes 6:9 *NLT*).

Did you know that if you earn $37,000 a year or more you are in the top 3% of the top income earners in the world? If you earn more than $45,000 a year you are in the top 1% of wage earners in the world! Most people in the world would say that you were rich. I think sometimes we get so busy working for more that we stop being grateful for what we have.

GOD HAS GIVEN US EVERYTHING THAT WE HAVE AS A GIFT.

Of course, there's no reason to feel guilty about our relative prosperity—instead, we should be grateful for what we have! We know the Bible says, *"Every good gift and every perfect gift is from above"* (James 1:17 *NKJV*). If someone gives you a gift should you feel guilty? No! God has given us everything that we have as a gift. Let's stop looking at what we don't have and starting thanking Him for what we do have!

Fight the current of discontentment! Every day we see thousands of advertisements telling us we need stuff to be happy. Yet, how many of those things that we "need" to be happy weren't in existence twenty years ago? We won't be happy without that iPod/iPhone/iPad, but just a few years ago they didn't even exist. That advertisement is lying to you if it says your next purchase will finally bring you happiness!

Our desire for bigger and better is an appetite—and appetites are never fully satisfied. You don't eat one great meal and then never eat another meal again. By definition, our appetite for things is never fully satisfied. For example, the last time my family bought a house, we thought, "This is it! This is finally it!" Then we visited some friends in their new house—and all of a sudden we started saying things like, "In our next house…"

Although it seems like the best way to satisfy an appetite is to feed it, the truth is that the more you feed it, the more hungry you get—the more you have, the more you want. Of course, our culture encourages us to feed the appetite. But the cure is to *starve* the appetite.

"Now godliness with contentment is great gain" (1 Timothy 6:6 *NKJV*).

For our culture, "great gain" is getting more stuff. But God has redefined "great gain" for us—it's more than just stuff. Godliness combined with thankfulness for what we do have is true gain. If our culture is right and gain is only about getting stuff, then when we die we will have gained nothing.

"Command those who are rich in this present age not to be haughty, nor to trust in uncertain riches but in the living God, who gives us richly all things to enjoy. Let them do good, that they

be rich in good works, ready to give, willing to share, storing up for themselves a good foundation for the time to come..." (1 Timothy 6:17-19 *NKJV*).

What if we focused on becoming rich in our good works? What if we invested our lives in God's work by getting to church every week and faithfully serving in ministries that helped others?

"No one can serve two masters. For you will hate one and love the other, or be devoted to one and despise the other. You cannot serve both God and money" (Luke 16:13 *NLT*).

Some people are serving money and not serving God. When they encounter a storm in life, they call out for God to save them—not so they can continue to serve Him, but so they can get back to serving their money. Are we really serving stuff and praying God will help us? God will not answer a prayer that would help someone put another "god" before Him!

How can we tell if we love money? Think back to when you were first "in love" with that special person. Can you remember doing some stupid things because you were in love?

Now think about your relationship with money. Have you done stupid things for money? Like walking down an aisle looking for things you don't know you need until you see them? Or purchasing things you couldn't afford on credit because you can't wait? Or buying something on credit that you no longer have by the time you finally pay it off? Or buying more house than you could afford so you could have more space to store the stuff you bought on credit but didn't really need?

"But you, O man of God...pursue righteousness, godliness, faith, love, patience, gentleness..." (1 Timothy 6:11 *NKJV*).

What are we going to look to for our source of joy and happiness? God isn't against money—He is only against money being our god. He wants to be God. He wants to be our Source.

"Their sorrows shall be multiplied who hasten after another god... In Your presence is fullness of joy; at Your right hand are pleasures forevermore" (Psalm 16:4,11b *NKJV*).

> GOD ISN'T AGAINST MONEY— HE IS ONLY AGAINST MONEY BEING OUR GOD.

Testing Your Heart

Fortunately, God has given us a test to make sure we are serving Him and not money. It is called the tithe. This isn't something God wants *from* you—it's something He wants *for* you.

"And in the process of time it came to pass that Cain brought an offering of the fruit of the ground to the Lord. Abel also brought of the firstborn of his flock and of their fat. And the Lord respected Abel and his offering, but He did not respect Cain and his offering" (Genesis 4:3-5 *NKJV*).

In the story of Cain and Abel, have you ever wondered why God didn't receive Cain's offering, but did receive Abel's?

Abel brought the firstborn and "of their fat" (meaning "the best").

Cain brought leftovers. God doesn't bless leftovers. He is God and worthy of our best. When we tithe and write our check we are saying, "God, I put you before the mortgage company, before the electric company and before the mall and Best Buy. You are first and foremost in my life."

> MANY CHRISTIANS ARE AFRAID GOD WANTS TO TAKE THEIR STUFF.

Many Christians are afraid God wants to take their stuff. But if God wants your stuff, do you think He has to wait for you to die to get it? Do you really think God is interested in your stuff? Have you read about Heaven? He uses gold as asphalt to pave His streets! He sits on a gold throne, while yours is porcelain!

The point is that He wants to be your God. He refuses to be second to the stuff He gave you. Giving is a test of our heart. God knows our heart by looking at our treasure.

"And how can we be sure that we belong to him? By obeying his commandments. If someone says, 'I belong to God,' but doesn't obey God's commandments, that person is a liar and does not live in the truth. But those who obey God's word really do love him. That is the way to know whether or not we live in him. Those who

say they live in God should live their lives as Christ did" (1 John 2:3-6 *NLT*).

In the Bible, numbers have specific meaning and significance. For example, "3" stands for perfection, "7" for completion, and "12" for divine government. The tithe is ten percent—which is the number 10. "Ten" is the number of testing.

How many plagues were there in Egypt that tested Pharaohs heart? *Ten!*

How many commandments are there? *Ten!*

How many virgins in Matthew 25 were tested to see if they were ready for God's return? *Ten!*

Every time we receive a paycheck God is testing our hearts.

So how well is the average Christian doing with this test? The statistics show that the average Christian gives two percent of their income. Less than three percent of us actually tithe.

Tragically, this means that most average Christians are not experiencing financial victory because they have fallen victim to this tactic of the enemy at work against them.

"Therefore submit to God. Resist the devil and he will flee from you" (James 4:7 *NKJV*).

"Flee" in the original Greek language means "to run away in terror." When you open your checkbook, does the devil scream like a little girl and run? Or when you open your checkbook, do you scream—and the devil just laughs and does a victory dance?

This verse says that the devil should flee from our lives when we do something. Notice that this is a conditional verse. Of course, God's love is unconditional—but victory comes with conditions.

What is the condition in this verse for the devil to flee?

"Submit to God."

We will have victory in those areas of our lives where we are submitted to God. And the opposite is also true—in those areas where we are not submitted to God, the enemy has victory. The devil's tactic is to divide us from the strength of God. Where he has separated us from God, he can defeat us.

What does it mean to be submitted to God in the area of our finances? Let's take a look at scripture to see what God has established as His definition of submission.

> *"'Return to Me, and I will return to you,'*
> *Says the Lord of hosts.*
> *"But you said,*
> *'In what way shall we return?'*
> *"Will a man rob God?*
> *Yet you have robbed Me!*
> *"But you say,*
> *'In what way have we robbed You?'*

"In tithes and offerings.

You are cursed with a curse,

"For you have robbed Me,

Even this whole nation."

—Malachi 3:7b-8 NKJV

God says that submission to Him in our finances begins with us bringing into His house the tithe. God knows where our hearts are by where we put His tithe. Why should God give us more of His money if we are going to keep robbing Him of the tithe?

What is the tithe? The word "tithe" literally means "tenth." The tithe is a tenth of our income. Anything you give above your tithe is an "offering." The tithe belongs to the Lord. We often call tithing "giving," but actually tithing is returning to the Lord what already is His. We are managers of God's money, and He asks for ten percent—a tithe—back.

Whenever tithe is mentioned in scripture, it never says give the tithe—it always says bring the tithe. We are returning to God what is His. If I asked to borrow your coat, and for Christmas I gave you a box and it was your coat wrapped up, what would you think of my gift?

"Gee, thanks for giving me my coat back!"

GOD DOESN'T SEEM TO HAVE ANY TROUBLE TELLING US THE BENEFITS WE RECEIVE WHEN WE GIVE.

173

God, What's Taking So Long?

Doesn't it seem like we should have a higher motive for our giving than getting? But God doesn't seem to have any trouble telling us the benefits we receive when we give.

> *"Bring all the tithes into the storehouse,*
> *That there may be food in My house,*
> *And try Me now in this,"*
> *Says the Lord of hosts,*
> *"If I will not open for you the windows of heaven*
> *And pour out for you such blessing*
> *That there will not be room enough to receive it.*
>
> *"And I will rebuke the devourer for your sakes,*
> *So that he will not destroy the fruit of your ground,*
> *Nor shall the vine fail to bear fruit for you in the field,"*
> *Says the Lord of hosts;*
> *"And all nations will call you blessed,*
> *For you will be a delightful land,"*
> *Says the Lord of hosts.*

(Malachi 3:10-12 *NKJV*)

God says He will open the windows of His blessing to you. If Bill Gates said he were to open the windows of his checkbook to you, would you get excited?

This guarantee of blessing is so sure that God even says we can test Him on it. This is the only place where God says we may test Him—and we are encouraged to test Him. I

174

can hear God saying, "I dare you! Just try to prove me wrong in this! Bring it on!"

John Templeton, chairman of the Templeton Funds, once said, "I have observed over 100,000 families over my years of investment counseling. I always saw greater prosperity and happiness among those families who tithed than among those who didn't."

James Kraft, founder of the Kraft Cheese Corporation, who gave approximately 25% of his enormous income to Christian causes for many years, said, "The only investment I ever made which has paid consistently increasing dividends is the money I have given to the Lord."

God said He would rebuke the devourer. He will fight your money battles. He will place a blessing on what you have so that it will last even longer. God will be your Brinks truck to protect your money.

EVERY TIME YOU GIVE, IT'S LIKE GOD IS GIVING THE DEVIL A BLACK EYE IN THE AREA OF YOUR FINANCES.

But since God rebukes the devil when he tries to attack your finances, doesn't it make sense that the devil will try to talk you out of giving? The enemy hates it when you give! Every time you give, it's like God is giving the devil a black eye in the area of your finances.

When you give, you are investing in eternity. You can't take it with you—but you can send it ahead of you!

God, What's Taking So Long?

"Do not lay up for yourselves treasures on earth, where moth and rust destroy and where thieves break in and steal; but lay up for yourselves treasures in heaven, where neither moth nor rust destroys and where thieves do not break in and steal" (Matthew 6:19-21 *NKJV*).

Years ago, in one of her columns, Ann Landers printed a letter from a girl who said her uncle was the stingiest person she had ever met. For his whole life he had taken $20 out of every paycheck and hidden it under his mattress—and then refused to spend any of it, not even one dollar. At the end of his life, as the uncle lay dying, he said to his wife, "Promise me that when I die you will take all the money from under my mattress and bury it with me." The wife promised him that she would do as he asked.

Before long he died, and his wife kept her promise. At his funeral she dutifully placed a check for the full amount in the casket with him.

When you get to Heaven, which do you think is the most likely thing you will say to yourself: "Man, I just gave too much!" Or, "I wish I would have given more!"?

If you knew that tomorrow the American dollar would be worthless and the only money that would have value would be the Euro, what would you do? Wouldn't you run to the bank and exchange all the money you could?

When we give, our giving converts our money from earthly currency (that will one day be worthless) into an eternal currency.

Where do we pay our tithes? We saw in Malachi 3:10 that our tithe goes into the storehouse so there may be food to eat. We should tithe to where we get fed spiritually. Ordinarily, this will be your local church.

Everything you enjoy at your church has been paid for by someone's tithe. Ask yourself how your church would be doing if everyone gave like you do. Would your church be open and thriving next weekend—or would it have to close its doors?

Occasionally you'll encounter people who say we shouldn't tithe because tithing is part of the Old Testament Law and is not taught in the New Testament.

But this argument is wrong because the principle of tithing predates the instructions to tithe in the Law.

Abraham gave the tenth to Melchizedek 500 years before the Law. Jacob promised to give God the tenth 400 years before the Law. The tree in the Garden of Eden was God's tithe. Abraham offered his first-born son, Isaac, as a tithe and God gave Jesus, His first-born son, as His tithe—and the harvest He reaped was us!

Everything in the Old Testament is a picture of our life in the New Testament. The disciples met on Sunday, the first day of the week, to put God first. What is the first of the Ten Commandments? *"You shall have no other gods before me."* God refuses to be second place to anybody or anything.

God, What's Taking So Long?

The message of tithing isn't that we just give to get. The real and greater message of tithing is: "God, you are first in my life!"

Tithing really comes down to one question—do we trust God or not? Will we trust Him for our salvation, but not with our money?

"For I am the Lord, I do not change; therefore you are not consumed, O sons of Jacob. Yet from the days of your fathers you have gone away from My ordinances and have not kept them" (Malachi 3:6-11 *NKJV*).

Notice God says that He doesn't change and chooses to say that right before the message of putting Him first with our tithes and offerings. This is an eternal truth.

"Woe to you, scribes and Pharisees, hypocrites! For you pay tithe of mint and anise and cummin, and have neglected the weightier matters of the law: justice and mercy and faith. These you ought to have done, without leaving the others undone" (Matthew 23:23 *NKJV*).

Jesus didn't say, "Stop tithing! That is Old Testament law!" In fact, Jesus upped the ante. In the Law it said to not murder, but Jesus upped the commitment and said, "Whoever hates in his heart commits murder." The Law said not to commit adultery, but Jesus said, "Whoever lusts in his heart has already committed adultery."

Jesus didn't up the great commission and lower the church's funding to get it done. Just read the first few chapters of the book of Acts and you'll see that they had more than enough resources for the ministry and missions they had to do.

So if you haven't experienced the blessing of tithing in your life, what are you waiting for? God asks you to test Him in this. Personally, I have seen this work in my own life for over twenty years. I have never been able to out-give God. As a pastor, I have seen this work countless times in people's lives as they take the step of faith and tithe— and God meets them and proves Himself faithful time and time again!

Discussion Questions

1. Next month you're going to spend your money on your basic living expenses—perhaps housing, food, transportation, clothing, etc. Why would it be wise to have a predetermined spending plan?

2. Think about the things you've spent your money on over the past month or two and evaluate whether each of those expenditures was a "need," a "want," or a "desire."

3. Why can tithing be considered a "test" of your heart? Why would the devil want to keep us from tithing?

4. Will you be tithing on the money you earn next month? Why or why not?

CHAPTER THIRTEEN

Waiting for Your Healing

You may be praying about a health problem and wondering, "God, why is it taking so long for You to heal me?"

Over the years many people have come to me as a pastor and asked me to pray for their physical healing. My experience is that sometimes God heals them instantaneously and sometimes He heals them more gradually—and in most cases I have no idea why God chooses to deal with one person one way and someone else another way.

But I do know that it's in God's heart to bring healing to His people. We see this clearly in the ministry of Jesus. Everywhere He went, the Bible tells us, *"when Jesus went out He saw a great multitude; and He was moved with compassion for them, and healed their sick"* (Matthew 14:14 *NKJV*).

So what should you be doing after you've asked God to heal you or you've prayed for someone else?

I HAVE NO IDEA WHY GOD CHOOSES TO DEAL WITH ONE PERSON ONE WAY AND SOMEONE ELSE ANOTHER WAY.

First, begin thanking God. Thank Him for His love and His healing power. *"Whatever things you ask when you pray,"* Jesus said, *"believe that you receive them, and you will have them"* (Mark 11:24 *NKJV*). The Bible says, *"Do not be anxious about anything, but in everything, by prayer and petition, with thanksgiving, present your requests to God"* (Philippians 4:6 *NKJV*).

Second, begin meditating on God's Word. Read the scriptures that remind you of God's power to work miracles and His desire to heal you. To help you get started, here are some Bible verses that will build your faith and encourage you as you expect your miracle!

Some Scriptures about Your Healing

And behold, a leper came and worshiped Him, saying, "Lord, if You are willing, You can make me clean."

Then Jesus put out His hand and touched him, saying, "I am willing; be cleansed." Immediately his leprosy was cleansed.

Matthew 8:2-3 *NKJV*

Now a certain woman had a flow of blood for twelve years, and had suffered many things from many physicians. She had spent all that she had and was no better, but rather grew worse. When she heard about Jesus, she came behind Him in the crowd and touched

His garment. For she said, "If only I may touch His clothes, I shall be made well."

Immediately the fountain of her blood was dried up, and she felt in her body that she was healed of the affliction. And Jesus, immediately knowing in Himself that power had gone out of Him, turned around in the crowd and said, "Who touched My clothes?"

But His disciples said to Him, "You see the multitude thronging You, and You say, 'Who touched Me?'"

And He looked around to see her who had done this thing. But the woman, fearing and trembling, knowing what had happened to her, came and fell down before Him and told Him the whole truth. And He said to her, "Daughter, your faith has made you well. Go in peace, and be healed of your affliction."

> "DAUGHTER, YOUR FAITH HAS MADE YOU WELL."

Mark 5:25-34 *NKJV*

And behold, there was a woman who had a spirit of infirmity eighteen years, and was bent over and could in no way raise herself up. But when Jesus saw her, He called her to Him and said to her, "Woman, you are loosed from your infirmity." And He laid His hands on her, and immediately she was made straight, and glorified God.

But the ruler of the synagogue answered with indignation, because Jesus had healed on the Sabbath; and he said to the crowd, "There are six days on which men ought to work; therefore come and be healed on them, and not on the Sabbath day."

God, What's Taking So Long?

The Lord then answered him and said, "Hypocrite! Does not each one of you on the Sabbath loose his ox or donkey from the stall, and lead it away to water it? So ought not this woman, being a daughter of Abraham, whom Satan has bound—think of it—for eighteen years, be loosed from this bond on the Sabbath?"

Luke 13:11-16 *NKJV*

And again He entered Capernaum after some days, and it was heard that He was in the house. Immediately many gathered together, so that there was no longer room to receive them, not even near the door. And He preached the word to them. Then they came to Him, bringing a paralytic who was carried by four men. And when they could not come near Him because of the crowd, they uncovered the roof where He was. So when they had broken through, they let down the bed on which the paralytic was lying.

When Jesus saw their faith, He said to the paralytic, "Son, your sins are forgiven you."

And some of the scribes were sitting there and reasoning in their hearts, "Why does this Man speak blasphemies like this? Who can forgive sins but God alone?"

"JESUS SAID TO HIM, 'I WILL COME AND HEAL HIM.'"

But immediately, when Jesus perceived in His spirit that they reasoned thus within themselves, He said to them, "Why do you reason about these things in your hearts? Which is easier, to say to the paralytic, 'Your sins are forgiven you,' or to say, 'Arise, take up your bed and walk'? But that you may know that the Son of Man has power on earth to forgive sins"—He

184

said to the paralytic, "I say to you, arise, take up your bed, and go to your house." Immediately he arose, took up the bed, and went out in the presence of them all, so that all were amazed and glorified God, saying, "We never saw anything like this!"

Mark 2:1-12 *NKJV*

Now when Jesus had entered Capernaum, a centurion came to Him, pleading with Him, saying, "Lord, my servant is lying at home paralyzed, dreadfully tormented."

And Jesus said to him, "I will come and heal him."

The centurion answered and said, "Lord, I am not worthy that You should come under my roof. But only speak a word, and my servant will be healed. For I also am a man under authority, having soldiers under me. And I say to this one, 'Go,' and he goes; and to another, 'Come,' and he comes; and to my servant, 'Do this,' and he does it."

When Jesus heard it, He marveled, and said to those who followed, "Assuredly, I say to you, I have not found such great faith, not even in Israel! And I say to you that many will come from east and west, and sit down with Abraham, Isaac, and Jacob in the kingdom of heaven. But the sons of the kingdom will be cast out into outer darkness. There will be weeping and gnashing of teeth." Then Jesus said to the centurion, "Go your way; and as you have believed, so let it be done for you." And his servant was healed that same hour.

Matthew 8:5-13 *NKJV*

"AND THE POWER OF THE LORD WAS PRESENT TO HEAL THEM."

God, What's Taking So Long?

And Jesus went about all Galilee, teaching in their synagogues, preaching the gospel of the kingdom, and healing all kinds of sickness and all kinds of disease among the people.

Matthew 4:23 *NKJV*

Now it happened on a certain day, as He was teaching, that there were Pharisees and teachers of the law sitting by, who had come out of every town of Galilee, Judea, and Jerusalem. And the power of the Lord was present to heal them.

Luke 5:17 *NKJV*

And the whole multitude sought to touch Him, for power went out from Him and healed them all.

Luke 6:19 *NKJV*

And when Jesus went out He saw a great multitude; and He was moved with compassion for them, and healed their sick.

Matthew 14:14 *NKJV*

Now Peter and John went up together to the temple at the hour of prayer, the ninth hour. And a certain man lame from his mother's womb was carried, whom they laid daily at the gate of the temple which is called Beautiful, to ask alms from those who entered the temple; who, seeing Peter and John about to go into the temple, asked for alms. And fixing his eyes on him, with John, Peter said, "Look at us." So he gave them his attention, expecting to receive something

"IN THE NAME OF JESUS CHRIST OF NAZARETH, RISE UP AND WALK!"

from them. Then Peter said, "Silver and gold I do not have, but what I do have I give you: In the name of Jesus Christ of Nazareth, rise up and walk." And he took him by the right hand and lifted him up, and immediately his feet and ankle bones received strength. So he, leaping up, stood and walked and entered the temple with them—walking, leaping, and praising God. And all the people saw him walking and praising God. Then they knew that it was he who sat begging alms at the Beautiful Gate of the temple; and they were filled with wonder and amazement at what had happened to him.

Acts 3:1-10 *NKJV*

Surely He has borne our griefs

    And carried our sorrows;

    Yet we esteemed Him stricken,

    Smitten by God, and afflicted.

But He was wounded for our transgressions,

He was bruised for our iniquities;

The chastisement for our peace was upon Him,

And by His stripes we are healed.

"AND BY HIS STRIPES WE ARE HEALED."

Isaiah 53:4-5 *NKJV*

When evening had come, they brought to Him many who were demon-possessed. And He cast out the spirits with a word, and healed all who were sick, that it might be fulfilled which was spoken by Isaiah the prophet, saying:

God, What's Taking So Long?

"He Himself took our infirmities
And bore our sicknesses."

Matthew 8:16-17 *NKJV*

For to this you were called, because Christ also suffered for us, leaving us an example, that you should follow His steps:

"Who committed no sin,

Nor was deceit found in His mouth";

who, when He was reviled, did not revile in return; when He suffered, He did not threaten, but committed Himself to Him who judges righteously; who Himself bore our sins in His own body on the tree, that we, having died to sins, might live for righteousness—by whose stripes you were healed.

1 Peter 2:24 *NKJV*

"For assuredly, I say to you, whoever says to this mountain, 'Be removed and be cast into the sea,' and does not doubt in his heart, but believes that those things he says will be done, he will have whatever he says. Therefore I say to you, whatever things you ask when you pray, believe that you receive them, and you will have them."

Mark 11:23-24 *NKJV*

"FOR I AM THE

LORD WHO

HEALS YOU."

"If you diligently heed the voice of the LORD your God and do what is right in His sight, give ear to His commandments and keep all His statutes, I will put none of the diseases

on you which I have brought on the Egyptians. For I am the LORD who heals you."

Exodus 15:26 *NKJV*

"And the LORD will take away from you all sickness, and will afflict you with none of the terrible diseases of Egypt which you have known..."

Deuteronomy 7:15 *NKJV*

"So you shall serve the LORD your God, and He will bless your bread and your water. And I will take sickness away from the midst of you. No one shall suffer miscarriage or be barren in your land; I will fulfill the number of your days."

Exodus 23:25-26 *NKJV*

O LORD my God, I cried out to You,
   And You healed me.

Psalm 30:2 *NKJV*

"He shall call upon Me, and I will answer him;
   I will be with him in trouble;
   I will deliver him and honor him.
   With long life I will satisfy him,
   And show him My salvation."

Psalm 91:15-16 *NKJV*

Bless the LORD, O my soul,
   And forget not all His benefits:

God, What's Taking So Long?

Who forgives all your iniquities,
Who heals all your diseases.
Psalm 103:2-3 *NKJV*

He sent His word and healed them,
And delivered them from their destructions.
Psalm 107:20 *NKJV*

He heals the brokenhearted
And binds up their wounds.
Psalm 147:3 *NKJV*

"My son, give attention to my words;
Incline your ear to my sayings.
Do not let them depart from your eyes;
Keep them in the midst of your heart;
For they are life to those who find them,
And health to all their flesh."
Proverbs 4:20-22 *NKJV*

Heal me, O LORD, and I shall be healed;
Save me, and I shall be saved,
For You are my praise.
Jeremiah 17:14 *NKJV*

"For I will restore health to you
And heal you of your wounds," says the LORD.
Jeremiah 30:17 *NKJV*

"Behold, I will bring it health and healing; I will heal them and reveal to them the abundance of peace and truth."

Jeremiah 33:6 *NKJV*

"But to you who fear My name

> *The Sun of Righteousness shall arise*

> *With healing in His wings;*

> *And you shall go out*

> *And grow fat like stall-fed calves."*

Malachi 4:2 *NKJV*

"And these signs will follow those who believe: In My name they will cast out demons; they will speak with new tongues; they will take up serpents; and if they drink anything deadly, it will by no means hurt them; they will lay hands on the sick, and they will recover."

Mark 16:17-18 *NKJV*

God anointed Jesus of Nazareth with the Holy Spirit and with power, who went about doing good and healing all who were oppressed by the devil, for God was with Him.

Acts 10:38 *NKJV*

"The thief does not come except to steal, and to kill, and to destroy. I have come that they may have life, and that they may have it more abundantly."

John 10:10 *NKJV*

God, What's Taking So Long?

"Most assuredly, I say to you, he who believes in Me, the works that I do he will do also; and greater works than these he will do, because I go to My Father."

John 14:12 *NKJV*

"Now, Lord, look on their threats, and grant to Your servants that with all boldness they may speak Your word, by stretching out Your hand to heal, and that signs and wonders may be done through the name of Your holy Servant Jesus."

Acts 4:29-30 *NKJV*

Be sober, be vigilant; because your adversary the devil walks about like a roaring lion, seeking whom he may devour. Resist him, steadfast in the faith, knowing that the same sufferings are experienced by your brotherhood in the world.

1 Peter 4:8-9 *NKJV*

Therefore submit to God. Resist the devil and he will flee from you.

James 4:7 *NKJV*

"AND THE PRAYER OF FAITH WILL SAVE THE SICK, AND THE LORD WILL RAISE HIM UP."

Is anyone among you sick? Let him call for the elders of the church, and let them pray over him, anointing him with oil in the name of the Lord. And the prayer of faith will save the sick, and the Lord will raise him up. And if he has committed sins, he will be forgiven.

James 5:14-15 *NKJV*

Waiting for Your Healing

Beloved, I pray that you may prosper in all things and be in health, just as your soul prospers.

3 John 2 *NKJV*

You are of God, little children, and have overcome them, because He who is in you is greater than he who is in the world.

1 John 4:4 *NKJV*

And he showed me a pure river of water of life, clear as crystal, proceeding from the throne of God and of the Lamb. In the middle of its street, and on either side of the river, was the tree of life, which bore twelve fruits, each tree yielding its fruit every month. The leaves of the tree were for the healing of the nations.

Revelation 22:1-2 *NKJV*

Discussion Questions

1. When we pray, why do you think the Bible says we should accompany our requests with thanksgiving?

2. God's Word, the Bible, describes itself as "living and active" (Hebrews 4:12). Why do you think meditating on scripture will help you get your prayers answered?

3. The well-known Bible verse, "by His stripes we are healed" (Isaiah 53:4-5; 1 Peter 2:24), is sometimes said to be about salvation and "spiritual" healing. What seems to be Matthew's understanding of this passage in Matthew 8:16-17?

4. When the leper approached Jesus in Matthew 8:2-3 and said, "Lord, if You are willing, You can heal me," what was Jesus' response? If you were to say the same thing to Jesus—"Lord, if You are willing, You can heal me"— what do you think He would say to you?

ABOUT THE AUTHOR

Erik Lawson is a 22-year ministry veteran noted for his unique ability to bring the Bible to life in memorable ways using vivid illustrations mixed with humor and practical life application. His down-to-earth approach, his genuine love for others, and his passion to see them experience a growing relationship with God is appealing to people of all ages and backgrounds.

Erik is presently the Senior Pastor of Element Church, a thriving congregation he pioneered in suburban St. Louis, Missouri, and his refreshing approach to ministry makes him a popular speaker across the country. For twelve years he was on the staff of Church On The Move in Tulsa, Oklahoma, with Pastor Willie George, where his forward-looking leadership style and outside-the-box approach was instrumental in helping their nationally acclaimed youth ministry, *Oneighty*, reach more than 2,500 students each week.

Erik has been married to the love of his life, Christy, for more than 17 years and enjoys spending time with their three children, Courtney, Brooke, and Wesley.